THE EXECUTIVE MYSTIC

THE
EXECUTIVE
MYSTIC

INTUITIVE TOOLS
FOR CULTIVATING
THE WINNING EDGE
IN BUSINESS

BARRIE DOLNICK

A HarperBusiness Book
from HarperPerennial

A hardcover edition of this book was published in 1998 by HarperBusiness, a division of HarperCollins Publishers.

HarperCollins books may be purchased for educational, business, or sales promotional use. For information please write: Special Markets Department, HarperCollins Publishers, Inc., 10 East 53rd Street, New York, NY 10022.

First HarperPerennial edition published 1999.

Designed by Laura Lindgren

The Library of Congress has catalogued the hardcover edition as follows:

Dolnick, Barrie.
    The executive mystic : psychic power tools for success / by Barrie
Dolnick. — 1st ed.
       p.   cm.
    Includes index.
    ISBN 0-88730-903-8
     1. Executives–Psychology. 2. Parapsychology and business. I. Title.
HD38.2.D645   1998
658.4'001'9—dc21   97-40275

ISBN 0-88730-954-2 (pbk.)

99 00 01 02 03 ❖/RRD 10 9 8 7 6 5 4 3 2 1

For my husband, Gero

CONTENTS

CONTENTS

❧ 2 ❧

CREATING YOUR PSYCHIC WORKSPACE:
Nontraditional Office Supplies

◈ 3 ◈

PERSONALIZED POWER TOOLS AND POWER CYCLES

◈ 4 ◈
PSYCHIC POWER AT WORK:
General Practices

❧ 5 ❧
PSYCHIC POWER
AND OTHER PEOPLE

◈ 6 ◈
PSYCHIC POWER TO IMPRESS

✇ 7 ✇

PSYCHIC POWER AND OTHER PEOPLE:

The Dark Side

◂ 8 ◂

EXECUTIVE ORACLES

One of my clients, Melissa, recently related a story to me that reminded me just why I wrote *The Executive Mystic*.

She described a meeting she'd had at her design firm the previous week, where she'd presented her ideas to a new client. The room was stiflingly hot; it was after lunch and her clients looked tired and distracted. Melissa's associates also sat in the meeting, shifting in their chairs and seeming equally uncomfortable. Melissa labored to keep her enthusiasm going while she explained her designs, but she became more and more drained of energy. She felt she couldn't get anyone to focus. She even tried to get the meeting going by asking questions and probing for more feedback. Defeated, she felt as if she had to prop up everyone's waning energy as well as convince her clients that her work was good.

In the end, the clients left, dissatisfied, dismissing the work by saying it wasn't really "on target," and asking for a new round of ideas in a week's time. Melissa was furious. Besides having to go back to the drawing board, she was angry that no one from her firm helped her out; in the meeting they just nodded, and afterward they simply plodded back to their desks.

When I heard this story, I thought about how vital psychic power tools are. Melissa could have easily infused the room with psychic energy, so that no one would have been tired. She could have used her tools prior to the meeting to electrify the atmosphere and prevent the midafternoon malaise. If she knew more about her own psychic power centers, Melissa could have also influenced both her coworkers and her clients enough to inspire a more spirited, productive discussion. Moreover, by employing some of the most basic psychic power tools, Melissa could have softened the resistance to her original work, so that it could be revisited rather than entirely discarded.

There is nothing more dispiriting—not to mention debilitating—than seeing your own hard work go unnoticed. Few of us can afford to have an important meeting go badly.

Everyone knows that today's world is more than competitive no matter what your industry. As technology provides faster, cheaper, and more convenient ways to do business, it is imperative that we keep up with it. As we struggle to manage these modern "conveniences"—voice mail, cell phones, faxes, E-mail, and the Internet—we are becoming increasingly divorced from our natural human interactive power: intuition. Additionally, the workplace is often muddled with emotional toxicity caused by other people's fear, hostility, and passive-aggressive behavior.

The Executive Mystic is intended to help you identify your personal power sources and tune in to the many subtle messages and energies around you. Through the use of psychic power tools you will be able to navigate through or avoid negativity, and magnetically draw in opportunity and success; you will also gain a better understanding of yourself and others, which will help you accomplish your goals, be they winning new business, acquiring a new company, or coping with a crisis.

Before you assume that this book isn't for you because you're not especially intuitive or because there's no room for "hocus-pocus" in your professional life, read on. Psychic power tools are for everyone, whether you're the chief executive or a temp. These tools can pave the way to a better, more productive workday and a more satisfying and successful career no matter what your field. So what if you're an ardent skeptic who wouldn't know an intuitive impression if it hit you in the face? Even better—because whether or not you want to believe it, even skeptics are constantly processing psychic information. With the help of this book, you'll be able to use that power to your advantage.

No, *The Executive Mystic* is not a ghost-busting guide for corporate America, nor is it an easy way to the top (although these tools will certainly help you get there). What it is, is a completely accessible and practical guide to getting ahead in business using intuition and other psychic power sources. Psychic power tools will help you attract opportunity, maximize quality in yourself and others, counter negativity from colleagues, plan more effective meetings, make better hiring decisions, build more productive teams, and increase your ability to cut through the constant clutter and distraction around you.

Whether you work alone or head a huge corporation, these tools can help you amplify the power of your workspace in order to become more creative. They will help you carry more personal power with you so you can make better friends and influence people. You'll learn easy ways to predict the outcome of your deals and negotiations, how to conduct a good meeting, and how to "psych out" coworkers and competition. With these tools, you'll find that your intuition is honed to a finely tuned frequency. It will also make you feel more accomplished, more confident, and more satisfied with your business life.

Let's face it: We've all said, before an important meeting or job interview, "I have to wear my lucky blue suit." Or "Tomorrow's a big day—better choose a power tie." What you may have dubbed as "superstition" is not so easily dismissed. It's no accident that the color blue enhances your ability to be clear and concise. Feeling more confident in your clothing can affect your body language, a tip-off to someone's state of mind and a commonly accepted power tool. So have no fear—using your psychic power will neither transform you into a late-blooming flower child nor turn you into an ardent New Ager.

Feel free to maintain a healthy amount of skepticism. I do. Because your psychic ability isn't a scientific (rational) power, there is no way to prove that psychic power tools really work except by your own successful experience with them. So try not to obsess over how and why these techniques work. Although I've tried to provide some explanations of the workings of psychic powers, you must, to some degree, suspend your desire for logic and proof. Trying to deduce the causes and effects of your psychic successes will only diminish the pleasure of your triumphs—and distract you from developing your power further.

The Executive Mystic will provide you with basic information to get you started, as well as techniques you can build on and practice with, especially in these first few chapters. Resist the urge to skip to the chapter you want to try first; it's important to understand how your own psychic power works and how you can use it to your best advantage. Once you've mastered the basics, though, feel free to enjoy *The Executive Mystic* as a handy desk reference for everyday use as various opportunities and challenges arise.

In addition, each chapter offers opportunities to practice your skills and to implement your knowledge, so you can test your newly improved psychic powers as you read along.

One last word: You needn't worry that becoming an executive mystic has anything to do with Faustian deals with the devil or becoming one of Satan's little helpers. The techniques, tips, and power tools described in this book are straightforward, time-tested, and supportive of life and free will. They cannot harm others, even in the most ruthless or difficult business deal.

The unconscious choices we make every day—from how we speak and what we say to how we forge alliances and when we initiate new projects—affect our business lives, negatively or positively, in big ways and small ways. This book will help you become more aware of the full range of your personal power and teach you to use it to your every advantage in achieving your goals.

ACKNOWLEDGMENTS

Thanks to my editor, Laureen Rowland, for her support, cardinal determination, and belief in *The Executive Mystic*. Thanks also to Lisa Berkowitz and Amy Lambo for working their magic.

Gratitude to Emma Sweeney, for her friendship and guidance.

I gratefully acknowledge the support and input from my teachers and fellow practitioners, Julia Condon, Donna Limoges, and Julie Winter.

I am grateful for the astute observations from executives Cheryl Callan, Alan Hammill, Marilyn Levey, Liz Nickles, Mary Lou Quinlan, and Ann Skalski.

Thanks for the support of my sisters, Randy, Amy, and Carol, and my mother.

And many thanks to my awe-inspiring clients for providing me with the enriching experience of seeing psychic power tools in action.

❧ I ❧

PSYCHIC
POWER TOOLS

INTRODUCTION

You may not think you are psychically gifted, or that you have the kind of time, energy, or concentration it takes to utilize a psychic gift. Allow me to dispel those beliefs. We've all got psychic tools, and we all use them, all the time. Most of us just don't know what we're doing.

Perhaps you are facing a meeting with your boss about your job evaluation. You know it's coming up so you think about it, wondering if it will go well, hoping that you'll be praised, or hoping that you won't feel too uncomfortable or be unfairly judged. That's nothing special—we've all been there, right? But what if I told you that just by thinking about the meeting, you are putting your psychic energy into it? And that if you had a handle on your psychic power tools, you could actually influence your evaluation—even before the meeting occurs.

It's true. You could turn your subtle wish—"I hope it goes well"—into a real blast of energy that could affect the whole outcome of your conversation. Once you've identified your personal power sources, you can actually send psychic energy into the future—to diffuse any potential unpleasantness and even to amplify praise. You can also use your power tools in the midst of a meeting. Rather than simply wish you had a better rapport with your boss, you can evoke a sense of calm, make a compatible connection, and diffuse any hierarchical energy that may negatively affect your discussion. You'll even get used to switching emphasis with different power tools while you're in a meeting—just try not to react out loud when you see how effective they are (as I did when first practicing with my power tools).

Mastering psychic power tools can make dealing with people, even difficult personalities, more interesting, less stressful, and perhaps even enjoyable. Psychic power tools get results. You can infuse a project with so much psychic energy that it comes to fruition even against great odds. You can turn a potentially hostile meeting or a hard sell into a win-win situation, ease your way through what you thought would be a tough negotiation, and create a more pleasant and productive work environment for all.

As you become more comfortable with your power, you'll find that you aren't pushed around by other people as much, nor are you at the mercy of events beyond your control. You'll find change exciting, not threatening and dark. You may even find that you welcome certain challenges, taking the opportunity to practice with your power tools.

The tips, techniques, and exercises in this book are designed to help you identify your power and use it more effectively. Before you can do so, however, you must take a moment to consider how much (or how little) you know of your own psychic gifts.

Understanding Your Personal Power

Consider the following: What does power mean to you? Abundance? Recognition? Influence? Wealth?

Do you know the difference between personal power and political power?

Physical power and material power?

Intellectual power and intuitive power?

How open are you to your own power?

How do you see power in others?

Do you move with your power at all times or is it halted or exalted depending on where you are?

How in touch are you with your own power?

Take this simple quiz to determine your Working Power Quotient. Remember, there are no right or wrong answers here—this is simply a test to assess your current behavior and get you thinking about the real *power* arena, away from what is expected in your work environment or what you have been told by others.

WHAT'S YOUR WORKING PSYCHIC POWER QUOTIENT?

Answer *a* (not at all), *b* (sometimes), or *c* (always) to these questions. Be honest!

_____ 1. In a crisis, I'm the person others come to for advice.

_____ 2. I dislike having to present my ideas to more than one person.

_____ 3. When I disagree with someone, I keep it to myself.

_____ 4. When the company does well, I feel I've contributed to it.

_____ 5. I often "feel in it in my bones" when change is afoot.

_____ 6. I cancel job interviews and meetings when I don't feel well.

_____ 7. I detest last-minute changes.

_____ 8. I don't like asking for a raise or promotion.

_____ 9. I can feel comfortable in most situations.

_____10. When things get really busy, I get really stressed.

_____11. I find that some coworkers tire me out.

_____12. I consider myself creative.

_____13. I believe in "paying your dues" whenever you start anything new.

_____14. I can tell the mood of a room right when I walk in.

_____15. I think that if you can't prove something, it doesn't exist.

ANSWER KEY

1: a=0; b=2; c=0.

Your psychic power will attract people in a crisis because they'll want your insight, yet it is best to choose just when you allow people to use your energy. You may need to conserve it for your own use.

2: a=2; b=1; c=0.

Speaking in public is rarely a problem for a psychically powerful person. You'll soon learn to use psychic power tools to calm yourself down and to captivate your audience.

3: a=1; b=2; c=0.

Psychically attuned people can discern when it is best to disclose differing opinions and when they are best left unsaid. It is never a good idea to keep things to yourself at all costs for fear of diminishing your power. Practice taking risks based on gut instincts and you'll start to trust your intuition.

4: a=0; b=1; c=2.

Executive mystics know that they have an effect on everything the company does, even in the most indirect manner. Take credit where it is due, and often.

5: a=0; b=1; c=2.

Your bones may be kinesthetic mechanisms for feeling the future. Those who heed their hunches, even via twinges of rheumatism, may be more prepared for the future and thus more powerful.

6:   a=1; b=1; c=2.

Odd as it may seem to you, your physical health has a direct impact on your psychic and intellectual energy. If you are under the weather, the best course of action is to cancel an important meeting; your physical and psychic strength are inextricably linked, and you won't be able to summon your powers to their greatest potential if you're not well. If you absolutely must go through with the meeting, I'll give you some hints to facilitate your performance.

7:   a=2; b=1; c=0.

A practiced mystic knows that last-minute decisions are part of everyday life and is secure enough to roll with sudden change. The more you grow into your psychic power, the less these shifts of fate will bother you.

8:   a=2; b=1; c=0.

If you find it hard to ask for what you want, you are less likely to get it. Psychically powerful people can comfortably request recognition and rightful compensation, and still be liked and respected by bosses and coworkers.

9:   a=0; b=1; c=2.

Psychic power can bring you much comfort in tense situations; it can also help you assume a chameleonlike quality so that you can blend into different environments. Even in an uncomfortable situation, you can conjure an atmosphere of belonging so that you are perceived to be at ease.

10:   a=2; b=1; c=0.

When things get really busy, executive mystics get really excited. There's a lot of potential opportunity in a high-energy workplace, and rather than feel stressed, the psychically powerful person senses a healthy challenge ahead. Unless you are physically unwell, being busy should equal having fun.

11:   a=2; b=1; c=0.

At some point, we all fall prey to toxic coworkers who dump their work, their negativity, and their anxiety all over our desks. If you feel drained after helping people out, don't do it again. Send them somewhere to learn the skills they need, rather than fuel them with your own good energy.

12: a=0; b=1; c=2.

Every single one of you should have answered *c* to this statement, because next to psychic power, creativity is a quality we all have in abundance. Yet it's a quality few feel worthy to claim. Psychic power is all about conjuring energy to create and implement your reality. If this concept is foreign to you, it won't be for long.

13: a=2; b=0; c=0.

Magicians and mystics hardly give a thought to how other people do things. Power moves at its own pace, sometimes on a different track, like the fast track. Don't get trapped by limitations that may not apply to you.

14: a=2; b=1; c=0.

The ability to read atmosphere is an extremely useful psychic power tool. If you have this intuitive barometer working for you already, you are well on the way to being a great success.

15: a=2; b=1; c=0.

Your psychic power may not be tangible, but it is very real. The evidence of your psychic power exists in the results you'll see from using it. Go on. Try it out.

SCORING

0-10: You're probably overthinking things. Your psychic power is a natural process that will take over when you relax your rules.

10-20: You have very good psychic potential, and power tools will help you hone your skills even more.

20-30: You're practically a practicing mystic, but you may learn a few new tricks from reading further.

⚛

Personal power is being able to create and live the life you want—and not be afraid to enjoy it.

⚛

Your power can manifest itself in relationships, accomplishments, possessions, experiences, and yes, money. But it is more than just money. Power is your real currency for maximizing the opportunities you have in life.

There are modern mystics among us. To some, Bill Gates wields strong psychic power because of his ability to invent, foresee, and implement his ideas. President Clinton is another man who demonstrates keen psychic power; beyond his extraordinary ability to smile, press his agenda, and react to insults with grace, his personal presence is reportedly so powerful that you can "feel" his charisma as he enters a room. But charisma alone does not powerful make; psychic power is best seen in the results of an individual's intention rather than in a powerful aura.

The Elements of Personal Power

Your personal power is composed of many parts: your voice, your looks, your personality, your ideas, and the ways in which you present all of the former. To better understand power, you can think about it using four categories that reflect the four basic elements: fire, earth, air, and water. Get used to using the elements as guides for definition—they are one of the keys to unlocking psychic power and manifestation, so you'll be seeing a lot of them. Here's a breakdown of what they stand for:

> *Fire represents your creativity, passion, courage, and aggression.*

Earth symbolizes your physical body, health, relationship to prosperity, and groundedness.

Air stands for your intellectual power, thought processes, and ability to communicate.

Water evokes the power of your emotions, intuition, and nurturing ability.

Each element has a different dimension of psychic power. That is, your fire element can work to fuel your courage or your will; just try breathing in some sunlight and see how you feel. Your body and its physical energy give you the power to relate to and attract prosperity. Psychic energy from your air element derives new ideas and facilitates nonverbal communication. And psychically, your water element provides you with a constant flow of intuitive knowledge, which you can access at all times. You may already make decisions using your gut instinct or your intuition, but if not, you'll learn to access and draw on these elemental powers through simple exercises described later in this book.

The only challenge to using your psychic power is remembering to call upon it. You have to use it consciously in order to reap its rewards, which is what *The Executive Mystic* will help you do.

Tapping into Your Psychic Sensitivity

You probably have had experiences where you knew the phone would ring, or when you just knew a meeting would be canceled. This is your psychic sensitivity operating on low power, when occasional impressions reach your conscious mind.

Psychic power adds a layer to your personal power that is unseen and unmeasureable, but very influential and very much there. A combination of your sensitivity and your ability to make use of your impressions, psychic power encompasses both your ability to exert influence and your capacity to read it in others.

For instance, you can tune in to people. Think of the last time you tried to persuade someone to come around to your idea, or to sell someone your product or service. Often, as you begin your conversation, you get immediate impressions about his or her reactions. You may sense that it's best to take a relaxed stance versus a hard sell, or you may know that your audience would better respond to a logical, emotion-free appeal. It's not that you could *prove* anything with physical evidence—you just sense the need to use a better tactic. That perception, that internal hunch, is psychic sensitivity. When you feel that pull, you are consciously experiencing your psychic power.

When you are sitting at your desk or in your office and others visit you, they perceive you on a psychic level, in part because the colors, materials, and arrangements of items in your office send psychic messages to them, contributing to their perceptions of you. We all send and receive psychically charged signals a thousand times a day. Just imagine if you actually knew what you were reading and saying—and how to use this power to your advantage.

Psychic Power: Moving Beyond the Obvious

Using your psychic power effectively can be instrumental to achieving your lifelong goals. By developing this natural gift, you will no longer feel compelled to limit your own accomplishments, nor will you still feel frustrated or unfulfilled, particularly when you see the positive effects of employing psychic power tools. Not only will psychic power tools fill you with clarity and confidence, they will enable you to affect your experience in many other ways, such as:

- Lowering the amount of negativity you are exposed to
- Increasing your influence in meetings
- Altering a coworker's behavior toward you, or opinion of you
- Waking up your boss to your new ideas
- Embracing new challenges with excitement
- Configuring a more effective and cohesive work team
- Distancing yourself from office politics and personality problems

❧

Psychic power is the ability to sense and see beyond physical reality, to remove the barrier of time and to shift or influence events accordingly.

❧

See the past, present, and future more clearly and more objectively. Draw in what you want, and avoid what you don't. Because psychic power is much bigger than your individual power—your psychic power is hooked up to the "cosmic hard drive"—you're endowed with the benefit of universal power, too. Once you master the use of the tools in this book, you'll be able to make better choices in business and in life; you'll be more conscious of what you are doing and how you are living, and not be as affected by other people's problems or fears.

One of the great benefits of using psychic power is that you yourself will feel less fear. The more psychically attuned you become, the more open, relaxed, self-reliant, and self-assured you will be. Such qualities will allow you to be creative, resourceful, and successful even if everyone around you is in full panic mode.

In addition to finding your psychic center, you'll also learn to keep your "psychic knees bent," making you more aware of change as it is approaching and less likely to be bowled over by it.

Turning On Your Psychic Power

Whether or not you believe it, your psychic power is inborn. Power tools will simply help you access your own power, use it consciously, and live more richly.

How You Know What You Know

You may be wondering, quite reasonably, how our twentieth-century minds can react to a collection of power tools that draw upon the elements of nature, and benefit accordingly. The great psychologist Carl Jung theorized that we tap into the "collective unconscious," a pool of universal symbols and common knowledge that has been passed down to human beings since the beginning of the human race. This would imply that we each know a lot more than we're cognizant of, and that we draw upon this source constantly.

Another similar theory is based on psychic inheritance. Everyone agrees that your physical genes come from your parents, their parents, and so on through history. But we also have a psychic heritage, bequeathed to us by our families, and frequently documented throughout history by mothers, sisters, and daughters in the form of letters and journals. Our psychic heritage is also influenced by our past lives, if you choose to believe in reincarnation, accounting for our unconscious recognition and interpretation of symbols, images, objects, and even people we've never seen before.

But How Do You Know It Works?

You well may wonder if these tools are helping you at all, and how they work in the first place. Skeptical or not, those are damn good questions, the answers to which are: Yes, they really work; you know because you can see concrete results in the quality of your work, your interactions, and your success-to-failure ratio. But even the most learned and esteemed experts can only guess at how these tools *really* work.

The interpretations of these tools have been around since ancient times. Animal symbols, colors, shapes, and natural objects have held very specific and individual meanings in our Western culture. Interestingly—and not surprisingly—Eastern cultures often interpret the same symbols differently.

In many cases, I have drawn on the wisdom of the Native American cultures, because it is most fitting with our country's energy, but I have included some representation of Eastern philosophy and some earth-focused traditions in this book.

If you're not unfamiliar with this type of material, you may find that some of the concepts in this book are already known to you. This may be for several reasons. First, psychic practices are virtually the same in any culture. You might find that your grandmother's folklore or religious rituals resemble some of the power tools. That's because these practices are all from the same power source. Second, lots of these techniques may make sense to you on a very basic level. That's because learning to tap into your psychic power isn't like learning a foreign language—you already have the resources, you just need a few tips on learning how to utilize them. You may use this book just to reactivate your psychic memory, and then you'll be surprised to learn how easy it is to go from there.

In addition, much of my research draws from the experiences of my clients, who have shared their highly valuable, real-life stories of using their psychic power tools at work. I also have consulted many excellent reference sources available on the powers of plants, colors, symbols, and various power objects in order to present you with relevant, practical, and easy-to-use techniques that will help you open up your psychic power flow.

Why You Don't Use Your Psychic Power

I hope by now that you're intrigued by the workings of psychic power, but you must be wondering why on earth you haven't been taking advantage of this power all along. One reason is that most of us have involuntary screening processes, such as denial, distraction, and fear, that prevent us from honing our psychic skills. These shields prevent us from getting really good psychic information and keep us from using our psychic influence effectively. Another reason is that our parents, our friends, and our society, for the most part, condition us not to take psychic power and phenomena seriously. Still another reason is that if we are not trained to exploit these power sources, we can't possibly know what we're missing by not using them.

In helping you prepare for the tips and tools found in this book, let's look at the three most common screening processes, with an eye toward removing them.

DENIAL Some of our reluctance to process psychic information consciously is because of denial. You may sense, for example, that a problem exists or that something is about to go wrong, but you don't want to admit it. Once a client of mine sensed there was going to be high percentage of returns on his initially high sales. He was concerned about this hunch, and said he had no reason to think this way, which made him reluctant to act on it. After all, he reasoned, there was no rationale for taking his sales projections down. I recommended that he follow his instincts and adjust his sales figures accordingly—he would always look like a hero if his hunch was wrong. In the end, he preferred the "head in the sand" technique. Of course, he had a monstrous time at the end of the year when, as he expected, the returns poured in and left him with a huge sales shortfall.

You may at first feel a little squeamish about going with your gut, but once you've done it a few times—and found that your intuition was right on the money—you'll find that it's not so hard. Today's business world welcomes people with "good instincts" and "keen insight." And the good track record your psychic power brings you will only reinforce the corporate world's value of on-target intuition.

Denial also occurs when we don't want to deal with some-one else's challenge or fear, so we simply shut our psychic sense down. The trouble is that nine times out of ten, our denial of that message only serves to delay (and sometimes fuel) future unpleasantness. Remember, psychic power tools can help you get a better grip on other people, from your boss to your coworkers to your clients, and turn them into benign competition rather than feared rivals.

DISTRACTION More commonly, there is just too much going on for us to consciously process all the psychic messages we're receiving. It's hard enough just dealing with voice mail, E-mail, and cell phones. A practiced executive mystic will be able to turn off the distraction, if only for a moment, to collect him- or her-self and "center" the energy. If you're a CEO or senior-level executive of a corporation, you probably have the luxury of support staff to shield you from the ongoing din; take advantage of it. Most of us, however, have to answer our own phones, letters, and faxes. This book will show you that you don't have to turn them off (literally)—you just need to summon the power to ignore them once in a while. You can be sure that the best psychic information you'll ever receive will come to you without a telecommunications device.

FEAR No one wants to hear bad news, so some of us just don't look for it. Much as we close our eyes in a horror movie, we can shut off our psychic power circuits if we sense danger lurking. Unfortunately, in doing so, we shut off a lot of good stuff, too. I used to work with a woman who believed that if you find out what's going to happen in the future you'll just have more to worry about today. This kind of thinking must date back to the Greeks not wanting to annoy the gods. Why would the future not hold at least some good news, anyway?

If you fall into a fear of the future, you've already given away your ability to influence it. Psychic power tools can help you shape your future—so you can actually prepare for it.

And speaking of fear, just in case you fear being chastised or laughed at for using psychic power tools, just remember J. P. Morgan's attitude toward using astrology in business. When asked if all millionaires consulted astrologers, he replied, "No, billionaires do," for they are the ones who could obviously prove that success has lot to do with magic.

Why I'm Telling You This: My Psychic Résumé

I graduated from the University of Wisconsin at Madison with a bachelor's degree in business administration. The curriculum included all the usual business major's courses: accounting, corporate finance, statistics, management, and marketing. Yet there was one course offered as a half-credit elective that made all the difference to my education—and ultimately to my life. Few serious business students wasted time on half-credit electives, especially not one titled "Relaxation Techniques," but it was in this class that I learned to meditate, which is the cornerstone of psychic prowess.

Now, don't get excited—this *is* a business book, and I'm not going to demand that you meditate. However, I will strongly encourage you to do so if you want to be at the top of your psychic-power game. The stillness you experience when you are in a state of total relaxation will open you to much more psychic information and power than you have ever before felt.

My accidental meditation class was my entrée into metaphysical practice, but it didn't stop me from entering the advertising world in London and then New York. As an account executive, I rose, somewhat aggressively, through the management ranks to the level of senior vice president. Some of my colleagues nicknamed me "Barriecuda." I used my relaxation techniques to get me through various agency mergers, client losses, and other crises common to the advertising profession.

Yet, although I was pursuing the elusive good life as a Madison Avenue executive, I realized I was leading a surprisingly unhappy life in general. With some cosmic encouragement (this is a euphemism for unpleasant events that leave one feeling lost or sad), I began to meditate more seriously, and found a gifted teacher whose classes in the psychic arts satisfied my curiosity.

As I learned more about metaphysics, I gradually came to terms with how it worked for me and for my life. I was taught how to accept my gifts through psychic power tools, and how to best use them.

I took my knowledge to work with me and started to experiment. I placed crystals on my desk, set meetings by the moon's cycle, and used my intuition to more skillfully win arguments. I taught what I was learning to interested coworkers, and helped my clients with their problems if they asked.

One of my talents is in astrology and tarot reading. For fun, I would bring my cards to client dinners and read their futures. I can recall seeing a layoff in one client's future, and then helping to prevent it. I also saw new product failures, career changes, pregnancies—just about everything you can imagine.

Although most marketers are very conservative, my clients enjoyed the experiments and found they were actually very helpful. Their curiosity made it easy for me to see how psychic power tools worked for other people, often in business situations. Soon I took to reading cards for strategic planning sessions, sales meetings, even commercial photo shoots.

That's when I realized that this stuff really works as an empowering and successful business tool.

Although not everyone has a gift for reading the future, I've no doubt you'll find that you have some intuitive skill that will help you improve your work experience. Psychic power tools are very individual—what works to attract opportunities for you may not work for the guy in the next office. Practice as much as you like and discover what methods produce results for you.

And if you're thinking, "No way would this work in my business," think again. I have worked with clients in financial markets, health care services, restaurant and hotel management, science, marketing, sales, communications, fashion, interior design, antiques, sports, and myriad other industries. This stuff works no matter what your field because it is universal by its very nature.

Results Come in Mysterious Ways

As you will learn in the following chapters, there are many layers to psychic power tools and different ways to use them.

My client Rudy wanted to get promoted, so he was using his power tools to encourage people to perceive him as a leader. At the time, he was a sales associate for a corporate travel company, and after seven years in his job, he was tired of being passed over for management positions. His former boss had told him confidentially that he was not perceived to have the "gumption" for a leadership role.

Rudy tried out some power tools to amplify his fire energy (he figured gumption was closely related to courage) and carried some power objects—a gold coin and a lion's tooth—in his pocket to bring him success.

On one business trip, Rudy sat next to a stranger, an older business executive, and during the course of their polite conversation, he got a sign that his efforts were working. His short-term companion assumed he was a vice president, and assured Rudy that even if he was not yet at that level, he had what it takes. Of course, Rudy didn't take this as gospel, but he rightfully felt it was an excellent psychic signpost telling him to keep going. He did, and he got his promotion only three months later.

You may find that when you are attempting to achieve a big goal, your power tools don't work until you give up on them. There is an ironic little truth in this: You may have to surrender before you succeed. You can set up a situation, create energy around it, stack the psychic deck in your favor, and still feel incomplete from the process and unsure of the results. Then, just as you're about to throw up your hands and say, "This is just a bunch of hooey," and forget about it, everything works out. It is an unfortunately tiresome process but it is a Zen-like exercise in non-attachment that we Westerners often must go through in order to allow our psychic energy to work for us.

Amanda, another client, used every power tool in the book to try to get on staff as a writer for a television show. She amplified her creativity, carried her power objects, evoked her power animal, sent energy ahead of her to meetings, even wore the right colors, fabrics, and scents to attract success. During the strenuous process of looking for a writing job, Amanda made very real progress. She met with agents, writers, and producers, some of the most important people in her business, and submitted scripts and samples continually. Then she ran out of leads and steam. Even her psychic power tools and exercises couldn't rev up her enthusiasm or her belief that it was going to happen. She finally decided to throw in the towel and "keep her day job."

She spent a month telling people she was no longer pursuing a writing job before the phone rang and she was asked to contribute some writing for a new show. She spent a weekend working on this effort, only halfheartedly, and it showed. The studio asked her to revise it and offered to pay her a substantial amount to do so. This little perk reignited Amanda's enthusiasm, and her work on this small job eventually led to the staff writer's job she'd hoped for.

Pursuing a large goal, like changing a career or moving up in an organization, can be frustrating, but the rewards of the effort are often far greater than the pain of getting there.

The Dark Side of Psychic Power

You are probably familiar with dark psychic powers, like voodoo, curses, or the myriad other psychic manipulations introduced on television shows like *The X-Files*.

There is indeed a dark side to power, as there is a dark side to everything, but contrary to fictional fascinations, you will rarely, if ever, find a practitioner skillful enough to create worldwide havoc.

Using psychic power to consciously cause pain, to control someone else's free will, or to violate some law of nature are considered the darker arts. These practices do not support life or the greater good (which is the lighter side of psychic power). You can use your psychic power to your own end, whether or not it is for the greater good. You can choose whether or not to go for what you want regardless of consequences.

In spell-casting or hexing, there is a commonly held belief that if you put out negative energy, it will come back to you threefold. You can be sure that you are messing with your karma if your intentions are harmful or destructive. You can be sure, too, that you will suffer for it in some way.

This is not to say that you'll burn in hell if you choose to use your psychic powers for selfish reasons. There is no "wrong" here, but if you are selfishly interested to a point where you would harm or endanger others to get what you want, you are opening the door to bad energy coming back to you. The law implicit in any psychic practices is *you get back what you put out*. I've known people who have insisted they get their way, and they have suffered for it. One highly competitive female broadcasting executive I know threw a curse over anyone who stood in her way. Sure, she was successful, but she had a reputation for having no heart—and I'm not the only one who made the connection between her corporate karma and the fact that her firstborn child was born with a severe heart condition. Coincidence? Maybe, but not likely.

The voodoo practitioners who deal with heavy-duty curses and evil are aware that they will suffer a kickback in their profession, but do so anyway. (Go figure.) Their psychic power tools include dolls, pins, and chicken bones. I can't imagine that you'd be inclined to keep any of the above in your desk drawer, but hey, you never know. My advice is to stay away from such things.

I do not subscribe to or practice the darker arts of psychic power, and therefore you won't learn any here. However, I am familiar with the strong desire for revenge (particularly in business!), so I will provide you with some karmaproof ways to direct your anger at someone who has wronged you later in the book.

LOCATING YOUR PSYCHIC POWER
Your Internal Power Sources

Before we focus on external power tools, like setting up a psychically powerful office, allow me to introduce you to your already built-in set of power tools—your psychic power centers.

You were born with an internal psychic "hard drive," which

you've already begun upgrading by flipping on the switches of your intuitive knowledge. Psychic power tools can help increase that power.

What I refer to as your hard drive are actually the interactive psychic power centers of your body. These are sometimes called *chakras*, and they are both transmitters and receivers of psychic information. These power centers, which work all the time, are constantly sending out or taking in energy from other people or from the atmosphere around you, and in turn, send energy from you out into the world. Because these centers can easily get tired or overloaded, you need to know what they feel like so that you can tell if they are open or closed, overactive or underactive, positive or negative, and effective or ineffective. You need to know how to cleanse them (they get dirty every day and then don't work properly) and how best to use them (soon you'll be zapping people with your third eye to get their attention and commanding respect with a simple thrust of your power center). Using these centers is remarkably easy and effective for sending out specific signals.

Your seven main psychic power centers are the most important psychic powers you have in your possession because they are discreet influencers of how others perceive you and how effective you are. For example, you could be presenting an intelligent and persuasive argument to a client while your solar plexus, the power center of your body that holds your confidence, is showing signs of weakness and insecurity. These are mixed messages, inevitably picked up subconsciously by the client, and don't contribute to easy success. Once you learn about the power centers, you'll be able to control and check on them while you are presenting, to make sure they are working for you, not against you.

Chakras—what I call power centers—are defined in almost every ancient culture—our own Western version relates to both the Tibetan system and the Native American system. But before you strip-search yourself looking for these energy centers, you need to know what to look for.

Seven Centers for Your Psychic Power

While you do have many psychic power points on your body, these seven centers act as the switchboard for every other part. They literally run up the center of your body, from the base of your spine to the top of your head. Each center guides a different part of your psychic power and each emits its own message. Sometimes, when they are overworked, chakras are too open and can make you feel off balance. Conversely, there are times when one of your centers won't open, and that can make you feel stuck. Once you identify your energy centers, you can get the hang of using them—opening and closing them, for example, depending on what you need them for. When you've been cornered by the most "toxic" person at work, you'll be able to close your centers so you won't absorb his or her negative vibes. When you're shining in the spotlight, you'll be able to open all of your centers at will so you can be admired in full glory.

Each of the seven centers is associated with a color of the spectrum. You can use the colors to psychically enhance the energy coming from each center and to send psychic messages to other people (which will be discussed in greater detail in chapter 2). For now, find each center and pay attention to how it feels and how it reacts during your day.

THE ROOT CENTER Your psychic energy begins at your root center, where the earth's energy enters your body. This is at the base of your spine in the back and at your pubic bone at the front. This first center is your survival motivator. It literally enforces your will to live and procreate. It is a very basic force, not one that will serve you directly in business, but one that could prove very helpful for grounding yourself if you are threatened by a crisis. Because the root holds your survival instinct, if you ever feel threatened, the energy of this root takes over from all other centers. This center is associated with the colors black and red. (See the chart on page 26 for an overview.)

THE NAVEL CENTER The next energy center is called the navel center because of its location just below your belly button—or the small of your back. Your ability to assimilate information and emotions, as well as your sexual passion, come from here. This coincides with the organs found here—your intestines are located in this center (assimilation and release), as are your reproductive organs. After a tough day, you may find you're holding energy here by way of bloating or gas pains. This is a signal that you are not releasing the stress that you have experienced. Conversely, after a big win or an exhilarating experience, you could find your energy aroused here. This energy center relates to the color orange.

THE POWER CENTER One of the most important energy centers in your work life is the third center, your power center, located in your solar plexus, midback, or diaphragm area. Ulcers commonly occur among executives whose psychic energy is overloaded here. This is where you carry your influence and urge to dominate, and it is also where you take in others' psychic energy. As soon as I learned this, I began keeping my arm or some files in front of my diaphragm whenever I was in a touchy meeting or confronted by angry people! However, you may also get some signals from this center that will contribute to your intuitive knowledge, so you won't want to cover it up all the time. You can also use your power center to send energy in front of you when you're walking through a crowded street or airport. People will get out of your way from your psychic signal. Yellow is the color of the power center.

THE HEART CENTER The heart center is the fourth energy point and is the midpoint for the seven. It is located between your nipples on your chest, and is often tender to touch. This fourth center is not used often enough in business, as far as I can see, for the heart is your source of unconditional love and compassion. When you make decisions about your career and creative pursuits, you need to do so from this center to be sure you're making the right one. It is often hard to open the heart center when the power center is engaged in combat, but it behooves you to try. Your heart will never steer you wrong, whereas your third center will simply be fixated on wanting to resolve a power struggle, be it for your own good or not. The heart center relates to the color green.

THE THROAT CENTER Above the heart is the throat center, from which you communicate and express yourself. The throat center is, of course, powerful as it relates to speaking, writing, and clear self-expression. You would open this center widely in a big presentation, important sales call, when giving a keynote speech, or during a heated negotiation. Blue is the color of this center.

THE THIRD EYE The sixth energy center is the third eye, located just above and in the middle of your eyebrows. Your third eye is very important, especially in business, as it gives you your ability to visualize, create, imagine, and even see the future. Your third eye also contributes substantially to your intuitive knowledge. Often you can "see" something before it happens. When you're struggling to come up with an answer, you may find yourself gazing off into the distance without actually focusing. This is an unconscious use of the third eye, or what we also call the "mind's eye," and this technique can be very useful in long-range planning, problem solving, or brainstorming new ideas.

Computers seem to assault the third eye. I notice this while I write this book, and especially after playing a computer game. Staring too long at anything will leave an imprint on your third eye and impair your ability to see beyond it, thus diminishing your psychic sense here. Imagining the color purple, which is generally associated with this center, can clear out your third eye.

THE CROWN CENTER The last of the seven centers is your crown center. This is located in a ring at the top of your head. Your crown center connects you to the universal energy, the cosmos, or whatever you like to call the greater energy around us. This center gives you knowledge; it is linked to your brain, which brings you both your intelligence and psychic memory. When you "know" something, such as when you experience déjà vu or sense that the phone is going to ring, you are using your crown center.

When the lightbulb of inspiration appears over your head and you don't know what hit you, but you've been instantly illuminated with a new idea, you can thank your crown center. You can easily open this center to bring in more brain power, but you cannot command it to be productive. The ruler of your crown center is the universe, not you. The color of this center is white.

"Seeing" Your Centers

Now that you know where your seven centers are located, try to visualize them (you'll be using your third eye to do so). Each center has energy running through it, back to front and front to back. This energy is generally the color of the specific center, so the root is red, navel is orange, and so forth. All the time, every day, you are sending out energy through these centers, and in turn, receiving it from others. Fortunately, you can't actually see this exchange happening—but you can definitely feel it.

SUMMARY OF YOUR
PSYCHIC ENERGY CENTERS

CENTER	LOCATION	COLOR	ENERGY
Root	Base of spine/Pubic bone	Red/Black	Primitive urges, survival, grounding
Navel	Below the belly button	Orange	Passion, assimilation, tolerance
Power	Solar plexus	Yellow	Will, nerves, mastery
Heart	Between your nipples	Green	Compassion, unconditional love, peace
Throat	Throat, mouth	Blue	Communication, self-expression
Third eye	Between eyebrows, but just above	Purple	Visualization, intuition, imagination
Crown	Ring around the top of your head	White	Knowledge, ideas, thought

"Feeling" Your Centers

Here are some examples of how your psychic energy centers act in different situations.

- You've just met a new client and you felt an instant rapport. Your **root** center is wide open.
- You're discussing an upcoming meeting and you can already see the project happening. Your **third eye** is playing tricks on you.
- You receive a warm thank you note from a customer whom you treated with respect and kindness. Your **heart** center brings you pleasure.
- You're totally stressed out and you genuinely feel that you can't take one more thing. Your abdomen tightens and your **power** center says, "No more or you'll get an ulcer."
- You've been trying to solve a problem at work and the solution just "came" to you. Your **crown** center opened up.
- You finally cleared the air with your boss about an important misunderstanding. Your **throat** center was flowing with energy.
- Ever heard of having "fire in your belly"? You're totally turned on by the prospect of a new project; your **navel** center is impassioned.

These are only a few simple situations in which your psychic energy centers react with your physical reality. You can use colors and meditations to open up these centers, to ease them if they're stuck, or even to slow them down if they are overactive.

Working with Your Centers

Don't feel as though you have to "get your energy centers working" in order to benefit from them. They are always working anyway, and they automatically shift with your mood and your routine. No one has complete control of these energy centers all the time—not even a yogi master on a mountaintop. The more skilled and practiced you are, the more consciously and even more effectively you will use them, but there is no great need to worry about them all the time.

To start using your centers, you first need to clear them. This is a simple matter involving a shower or bath with sea salt. Just rub the salt on each of your power centers and they will be free from toxicity. I keep salt in my shower so that I can clear them every morning.

Practice is essential for finding and getting used to manipulating your power centers. You just need to find a quiet place and time—and I mean time, at least fifteen minutes. Also, nix the phones, buzzers, or people who could intrude on your peace. If this sounds like too much of a bother, think again. In mastering you psychic centers, you will be learning how to make meetings go well in the future, generate new deals and opportunities, keep your cool in tense meetings, calm other people down, even attract attention without lifting a finger. These centers are infinitely useful tools for making your work life productive and agreeable.

PSYCHIC CENTER PRACTICE

Sit with a straight back or recline, and one by one, starting with the root and working up, place your hand on each energy center. Visualize the color of the center passing through that point on your body. Feel the sensation, if there is any. Allow yourself to stay with each center for a few minutes. Pay attention to what you feel emotionally and physically, and what you think of when you're on each one.

Can you feel it at all? Does it feel hot? Is there movement or change? Does it change when you think of different things?

The more you feel each center, the easier it will be to access its energy and shift it to your needs. Don't expect to master this immediately; this exercise is just a test drive that will help you get to know your different centers.

Your Hot Zones

Don't be surprised if you can't feel anything at all in some places, or if you feel a lot in one or two. Most people favor certain centers. Your astrological sign may help you determine which psychic center is most active for you. Every zodiac sign is associated with an element, a body part, and a purpose that relate to your psychic centers. Your astrological sign will give you a clue to which psychic centers of your body will be easiest to work with. Take the hint—work on the centers that don't come naturally so that you can achieve stronger power balance and better results.

Fire signs (Aries, Leo, Sagittarius) are associated with the power, the navel, and the heart centers. Pay attention to the root, throat, third eye, and crown for better balance.

Earth signs (Taurus, Virgo, Capricorn) are more grounded, and relate to the lower three centers, the root, the navel, and the power. Your heart is probably fine, too, so concentrate on using the upper centers, the throat, third eye, and crown.

Air signs (Gemini, Libra, Aquarius) generally use their upper centers (throat, third eye, and crown). The heart center will be fine if you are not too stressed, so concentrate on opening the lower center, the power center, the navel, and the root. It's called being grounded.

Water signs (Cancer, Scorpio, Pisces) tend to be open to the navel center, the heart, and the third eye. You'll need to pay attention to the crown center and throat center for better self-expression, and the power center and root center for holding your ground under stress.

Take at look at the following chart for the centers most likely to be "hot" for you:

Aries: Solar plexus, root   **Libra:** Crown, heart
Taurus: Root, solar plexus   **Scorpio:** Root, navel
Gemini: Throat, crown   **Sagittarius:** Third eye, navel
Cancer: Heart, navel   **Capricorn:** Root, crown
Leo: Heart, power   **Aquarius:** Crown, third eye
Virgo: Navel, crown   **Pisces:** Third eye, heart

Psychic Toxicity and Hangovers

Just imagine how much traffic your power centers encounter on a daily basis and how little control you have over other people's energetic emissions. You are probably walking around with a load of psychic residue and you don't even know it. This grit, dirt, and dross from others (and your own toxicity, too) can inhibit your psychic power.

Clearing is necessary and can be very therapeutic, particularly if you are receptive to other people's toxic energy. If you happen to work with people who are angry, uptight, or bitter, or if you are working in an unstable situation, you can be affected by others' moods.

Psychic toxicity is apparent in headaches, stress reactions like stomachaches or indigestion, and other common discomforts we write off to stress. Try clearing your psychic centers with sea salt (you can always just rub it on if you don't want to take a shower) and see if it eases your tension.

Honing Your Psychic Skills

Having located your centers and, one hopes, cleared them, you can begin to tune in to their powers. To do this—to become a master of psychic power centers—you are going to have to do something very difficult.

Sit still.

Stillness is the only way you can really feel your centers and their power. More important, stillness opens you up to psychic impressions. The quieter you become, the louder your intuition and clairvoyance can be.

Sitting Still (without the TV)

If you appreciate how difficult this is, you are already showing promise. Real stillness is allowing your mind to quiet down (not to mention your phone, your kids, and your computer) while still remaining awake. Only when you are really still can you explore and practice manipulating your psychic energy.

The easiest path to stillness (and I use the term *easiest* loosely) is that of meditation. There are many forms of meditation that can lead you to stillness, some of which allow you to tune in to a sound or rhythm that helps numb your mind. Any way you get there is okay, as long as it is nonchemical (no drugs) and safe. Here are a few ideas:

1. Use a personal stereo and listen to one of these kinds of tapes.
   - Guided meditations
   - Tibetan chanting or bells
   - Drumming sounds
   - Ocean sounds
2. Close your eyes and listen to your breathing. Use breath as a focal point for your mind.
3. Close your eyes and visualize yourself in a trance state You can breathe colored light into each psychic center.
4. Chant or recite a mantra repeatedly until you feel in a trance state.

How Do You Know You're Still?

Good question. The thing about meditating is that you don't know that you've "gotten there" until you stop and come back to the "real world." You'll feel refreshed, revitalized, and sometimes a little spacey.

If you are in a trance state and you are feeling stillness, your mind is very likely to come along and say, "Hey! this is it!"—in which case, you will no longer be in a still state.

Meditation is called a "practice" because you never really get it right. You may have a great first experience when you try it, and then not be able to duplicate it for a while. It doesn't matter, though. Your attempt to find stillness is enough to start opening your centers to psychic impressions. Pay attention to those centers that are easy for you, because they will be the first to give you some psychic information.

When you are still, your psychic power centers can communicate with you directly. You may get a vision of the future from your third eye, your power center may open up to give you some insight into your current work, or your heart center may calm you down to give you new perspective on a problem.

The time it is most difficult to command stillness, when you're anxious, is the most beneficial time to try it. While a panicked or worried mind is not easy to calm, just finding your psychic centers will help tremendously.

Ready, Set, Grow

Getting your psychic power tools together may be the shrewdest venture you'll ever make, because it can cost you very little, and you'll reap infinite benefits. A simple investment of time, practice, and a few inexpensive supplies will make you a powerfully psychic influence throughout your day.

You'll find that not only is psychic power your second nature, but it is in nature, everywhere you look. You'll never look at an office, conduct an interview, or attend a meeting in the same way once you've harnessed the power of your own psychic nature.

⚛ 2 ⚛

CREATING YOUR PSYCHIC WORKSPACE

Nontraditional Office Supplies

A PSYCHIC WORKSPACE ASSESSMENT

How many of the following items do you have in your current workspace?

Fax

Artwork

Photocopier

Plants

Computer

Rocks

Photographs

Printer

Animal figurines or pictures

Feathers

Wood

Color (not including industrial gray, black, white, neutrals, wood, or metal)

Favorite objects

Phone

Flowers

Candles

There are business tools and there are psychic power tools. Can you guess how the preceding items divide?

Psychic power tools, contrary to what you might think, are not about turbans, crystal balls, or laserlike brain waves. They're about nature and using natural energies to our advantage.

&

Nature provides the psychic power tools, and technology provides convenience and efficiency. If you are operating without one or the other, you are underutilizing your power.

&

It's also not enough to just have natural stuff around you— you actually have to connect with it somehow in order to benefit from it.

Take plants, for example. Plants are common in offices, but if you've got plants in your space just because someone else put them there and you don't take notice of them, you probably aren't benefiting from them. If you're conscious of your plants and actually take care of them, your participation in keeping their energies healthy and alive becomes a psychic cycle of well-being. They will thrive alongside you, and their health emits psychically supportive—life supportive—vibes for you, too.

Some of us keep favorite objects nearby, like carved pieces of marble or wood. These are power objects, because they are made of natural substances, and impart their own energy, thereby enhancing the quality of your energy. When you're attached to a natural object of any kind, for whatever reason, it becomes a personal power object, one that contributes to your psychic and creative powers. The very reason you are attracted to something is an indication of your psychic relationship to it. For instance, I have a collection of small rocks shaped like hearts that I've found on various travels. When I found each of those rocks, I felt a sense of encouragement, a lift in my spirits, so I consider them power objects for good feelings. Crystals, rocks, and shells can evoke different emotions and energies, and can be used in your business life for a variety of situations.

Pictures of favorite places you've been, landscapes, and scenery are also psychic power tools. Some executives are energized and inspired by photographs they've taken on safari or hiking. Others enjoy being reminded of the view from the porch of their summer cottage. The feelings that these images bring out are helpful in amplifying your psychic energy. A friend in advertising used to keep a picture of herself hiking in the Grand Canyon on her desk. She claimed it gave her strength to persevere.

Candles and colors might seem a little out of place in the workplace, but both can contribute to a positive psychic undercurrent. The flame of a candle is excellent for raising your energy of will and force, and can also symbolize intellectual illumination and inspiration. Clients are often resistant to lighting a candle in the office, but once they try it, only good things have come from it.

Colors can evoke positive energy, and are used more and more skillfully to create a supportive work environment. Not long ago, hospitals realized that patients heal better in a bright, sunny environment. You, too, can benefit from colors in your office that make you feel confident, creative, and inspired. Even if your office dividers come in a color like institutional teal, you can supplement the energy of your workspace by choosing bright binders, memo pads, or blotters to add a little psychic sizzle to your office.

THE NATURE OF PSYCHIC POWER
Nature's Vibe

You are an organic being, a carbon-based, pulsing life-form that emits energy. Your office is likely to be made up of inorganic materials like plastics, veneers, chemical coatings, and lacquers. These substances are man-made, not organic, and therefore do not give off a vibe. Because inorganic substances are psychically dead, you can give off all sorts of creative vibrations but you'll still get nothing back. On a physical level, you may feel dazed and headachy, numb and exhausted. On a psychic level, there's no support, no input, no positive contribution.

All organic materials have some sort of vibration—from animals, vegetables, and minerals to mud, gravel, and sand, which technically may not be alive now, but once were, making them psychically powerful. A grain of sand could have been a part of a shell created by a sea animal. Mud was once a plant that died and decomposed into the earth. A stone may be related to an ancient landmass. These particles, no matter how small or dead they appear, have ancient memories. They carry with them more life experience than we have, and they can subtly vibrate their powers into our environment.

Organic vibrations emanate constantly, and because we can't hear them, see them, or touch them, we often forget they're there. Don't believe it? Do some field research and leave that all-too-artificial office at lunchtime for a visit to a park. How do you feel? Now, duck into a big department store. Notice the enormous difference in atmosphere. Do you feel tired, energetic, excited, or bored? The vibrations in each place add to or detract from your natural energy, and part of understanding psychic power tools is knowing how to avoid the detractors and surround yourself with the kind of energy that will let you work better and more effectively.

Consider the implications of creating a psychically supportive atmosphere—imagine the retailer who begins to work with psychic atmosphere improvements. We already see some moves in this direction—look at book superstores. They consciously create an atmosphere that encourages relaxation and thoughtfulness, like an old library (but one where you can talk out loud), with wooden chairs, breezy openness, and a no-pressure sales staff. Customers linger and buy, and come back for more.

By knowing which stones, colors, animals, and plants to use in your office, you can amplify your psychic power and create the atmosphere in which you work best. You can also adjust your environment to help you prepare for a difficult meeting, deflect negativity, or be more creative. Putting an amethyst next to your computer will help keep you feeling relaxed and at ease. Traveling with a clear quartz crystal can make a business trip seem like a breeze. Try keeping one of your favorite stones in your pocket when you leave town—it can make you feel at home, no matter where you go. Just having a little something on your person during a big presentation can make a difference. I use the scent of lavender to keep me calm and clear.

Working without some nature around you is working at low psychic capacity, thus diminishing your potential for achievement and satisfaction.

❧

Using psychic power is simply hooking up to nature's forces to evoke your most productive atmosphere.

❧

And because you weren't taught psychic reading in business school, now's the time to learn.

READING PSYCHIC SUBTEXT

Every day, we're confronted with thousands of psychic cues and messages that, unconsciously, we read. Our interpretation of these cues often colors our mood, hopes, interest level, and relationship to our work and other people. These cues and messages are everywhere—in people's homes (their decor, scent, color choices), offices (you're learning this), and out and around town (from ads and architecture to window displays and the weather).

Of course, to use psychic subtexts skillfully you need to be able to understand them consciously and individually. Just because you have something on your desk that's derived from nature doesn't mean it's always a good thing. For instance, back in my advertising days, I once received a Christmas present from my boss. He gave me a small silver (a natural metal) letter opener in the shape of a dagger.

The psychic subtext of this gift could be interpreted on two levels. One, this was a way of adding natural power and force to our working relationship. Or two, this was a way of posing some sort of challenge.

I actually did like the letter opener, but because I try not to play up my aggressive side it was not an appropriate message for me to have on my desk.

A knife is a fairly obvious symbol of aggression, but even if it weren't, your psychic sense would evaluate it on an unconscious level. This unconscious process of forming an impression can manifest itself in subtle ways. For example, one of my coworkers saw the letter opener and mockingly cut his throat with it. I took that as a sign that I did not want that thing on my desk any longer. Whatever my boss's intentions, I didn't need the psychic subtext of an aggressive, negative symbol in my face.

From a positively powerful perspective, my client Jane has a beautiful blooming rose plant in her office. This is not just a cheerful diversion amid the mounds of paper piled around her; it actually gives those who visit her a psychic lift. Blooming flowers are a symbol of spring, growth, and beauty. Roses, in particular, stimulate the heart center, thereby increasing the opportunity for compassion and joy. When I witnessed a potentially tense meeting take place in Jane's office, the rose plant did the trick. Jane was on the phone when two executives showed up hungry to tackle a disagreement with her. While they waited for her to finish her phone call, they "stopped to smell the roses," after which they seemed to soften up considerably. Jane was able to address their issues, and they were able to respond sensibly and sensitively.

POWER TOOLS

There are many different natural power tools that can enhance and expand your psychic power. Keep them in your desk, office, or briefcase for those times when you need an extra lift.

Crystals, Gems, and Rocks

Natural crystals are formed from organic materials subjected to varying heat and pressure. After thousands of years, these materials formed gemstones and semiprecious rock formations. Some of these stones are common, like quartz, and some are rare, like rubies, emeralds, diamonds, and sapphires.

Opinions differ on how crystal vibrations actually work with our psychic energy. One theory, an ancient belief found in primitive cultures across the world, correlates the stone's vibration and color to its psychic properties. Crystals grow with natural facets that jewelers cut and shape. These facets are seen to be the source of vibration, and different types of crystal have different facets that vibrate at different levels. The vibrations associated with each type of crystal depend on its structural makeup.

CRYSTALS, GEMS, AND STONES
AND THEIR PROPERTIES

Agate	Grounding
Amber	Ancient wisdom
Amethyst	Emotional spaciousness, intuition
Aquamarine	Calming
Bloodstone	Vitality, courage
Carnelian	Creativity, prosperity
Citrine	Self-confidence
Coral	Calming
Diamond	Self-esteem
Emerald	Heart energy, prosperity
Fluorite	Relaxant, optimizes energy overflow
Garnet	Vitality
Jade	Earthiness, wealth
Jasper	Physical body
Lapis lazuli	Psychic ability
Malachite/Azurite	Self-expression
Moonstone	Intuition
Obsidian	Protection
Onyx	Stress relief, negativity absorber
Opal	Protection
Peridot	Clarity, patience
Pyrite	Eases anxiety
Quartz	Clarity, focus
Rhodochrosite	Self-identity
Ruby	Confidence
Sapphire	Self-expression
Tigereye	Psychic detox
Topaz	Heals the past
Tourmaline	Dispels fear
Turquoise	Protection

Another theory relies more on the absorption and emission of light. Black crystals, like onyx, absorb light and don't emit much; onyx is known as an absorbing crystal and can be used to absorb negative energy. I give this to people who work in highly toxic work environments. Diamonds, on the other hand, emit lots of shine and are known for increasing self-esteem. A diamond's substance is also the hardest known to man, and so contributes to one's perseverance and endurance. Each crystal's color and light contribute to its psychic impact.

Some crystals may feel good to you, while others do not. Your personal reaction and intuition will guide you to the right stones. Don't force yourself, for example, to hold an amethyst if it makes you feel uneasy. However, if it doesn't bother you too much, you may want to carry it for its beneficial properties. Amethyst isn't my favorite, but I try to carry it on occasion because it's helpful with intuition. I don't really like the spacey feeling it gives me, so I use it only when I feel it's necessary. Remember, your own comfort level will dictate what's best for you and inevitably guide you to what you need.

When you put a crystal in your workspace or carry it on your person, its properties will emit a vibration, a psychic subtext, both to you and to those around you. It is very subtle so it won't be noticeable to others, but you may find yourself acting more in line with the crystal's properties. Carrying a bloodstone may make you more courageous, while holding on to a garnet can give your energy a lift.

Raw crystals are generally stronger than cut crystals (and definitely cheaper) because they have more facets intact, and no one has messed with their composition. Crystals with points, or tips that look like sharpened pencils, are considered the most powerful, because their energies converge at the point.

Not all crystals are really crystal; some are actually rocks. This is true for jasper, agate, jade, and lapis lazuli. Most of these rocks are good for enhancing your physical energy. If you're having trouble concentrating, hold on to some agate or hematite. You'll find yourself slowly coming back to earth. Jade and lapis can amplify your power of manifesting abundance.

And—before you run out to obtain some shiny new power tools, forget fakes. They may look good, but they won't do a thing for your energy. Remember, man-made materials don't contain any psychic power.

Herbs

This may seem hard to swallow (and you won't have to swallow anything, by the way), but certain herbs carry with them very useful powers. And you don't have to have an office herb garden to use them.

Herbs, like crystals, grow from the earth. Since early civilization, humans have used herbs in rituals and for remedies. Until recently, with the broad acceptance of alternative medicine and homeopathy, we'd forgotten how powerful they can be in everyday life.

For instance, chamomile, the herb you probably know more for its tea, is an excellent prosperity herb. Gamblers use it to attract money (just wash your hands with it).

Remember, too, that herbs were seen as significant, and burned as offerings in biblical times. The three wise men carried with them gifts of frankincense and myrrh, herbs that represent spirituality. Frankincense lifts an atmosphere and cleanses it of evil. Myrrh, burned as an incense, purifies the area and creates peace. Can you just imagine the kind of environment you could create if you cleansed the negativity from your offices or opened the atmosphere to peacefulness? You actually can do this, with or without burning herbs.

In consulting on premises for businesses, I almost always start with an herbal clearing—but rather than risk having the halls smell like a church, I use what many Native Americans used:

sage. The smoke of wild sage does smell a bit like marijuana, but its therapeutic atmospheric effects are worth the temporary odor. An herbal clearing will cleanse the atmosphere of fear, anger, sadness, jealousy, and other negativity. Sage acts much like frankincense and myrrh, by neutralizing the atmosphere and opening the room up to more positive energy, encouraging healthy interactions and enhanced clarity. If you're worried about doing this during office hours, try it after work or on a weekend.

There are many herbs that are easily available and simple to use. For instance, fresh basil can ease arguments, and lavender can soften people's hearts. I've used both to diffuse tensions with business associates. Sometimes it works just to carry a sachet in your pocket or put some in a bowl on your desk. (I'm forever pulling shabby bits of leaves out of pockets.) Try a whiff of rosemary or spearmint to clear your head when you're stressed out or on "information overload."

HERBS AND THEIR PROPERTIES

LUCK LENDERS	MONEY MAGNETS
Cinnamon (incense)	*(Carry in your pocket or*
Cypress	*place in your office.)*
Lotus	Almonds
Nutmeg	Basil
	Bergamot
MIND SHARPENERS	Cedar
Mustard	Chamomile
Rosemary	Clove
Spearmint	Honeysuckle
Walnut	Nutmeg
	Mint
	Patchouli
	Pecan
	Pine

POWER BOOSTERS
(Place in your office.)
Carnation
Ginger
Vanilla

NEGATIVITY
DEFLECTORS
(Carry or place in your office.)
Anise
Basil
Bay
Mint
Rosemary
Violet

INTUITION
ACCELERATORS
Celery seeds *(in your pocket)*
Cinnamon
Peppermint
Sandalwood *(incense)*
Thyme

Color

Each color of the rainbow has been associated with certain properties and characteristics since long before history was written down. Their meanings survive today, in part because they are so simple and obvious. For instance, black means mystery and the unknown. Red means passion and anger. Blue means clarity. Doesn't this make sense? You can't see in the dark. Blood is often used as a symbol for anger and passion—and on a clear day you can see forever.

Color is very important to the psychic messages you are sending out. It pertains to your clothing choice, your office decor, even your presentation style.

I like to wear a red suit for creative presentations to clients because I want people to be impassioned by the work I do. Conversely, I choose blue when meetings are more focused on marketing issues, as it sends a message of good communications. It is also fun to mix and match colors to see what happens—although I would think twice about that acid green color on heavy business days.

In terms of office decor, color can have a positive, uplifting effect if used appropriately. One West Coast movie executive chose to paint her office yellow, an excellent color to keep spirits high and send a message of success.

Now, you may not have the luxury of choosing the color of your walls, the wood for your desk, or the color of your furniture. But even if you can't permanently change what you're given, you can temporarily adjust it. I used to bring throw pillows to the office to brighten up the drab gray of my furniture. You can lay a rug down, put a shawl or a sweater around the back of your chair, or add a colorful museum poster to change the atmosphere from ho-hum to hot-hot-hot.

THE POWERS OF COLOR

Black	The unknown
Blue	Trust, intellect
Brown	Earth, fecundity, fertility
Gold	Sun, riches, divine power
Green	Nature, life and death combined
Gray	Neutrality
Orange	Flame, luxury, splendor
Purple	Royalty
Red	Fire, passion, ardor
Silver	Feminine force, virginity
Violet	Intelligence, knowledge, sanctity
White	Simplicity, light, innocence
Yellow (pale, the sun)	Success, light
Yellow (dark)	Avarice, treachery

Symbols

Symbols come in many forms, from hieroglyphs to the photographic images of real people, and speak a strong psychic language. The significance of symbols is thousands of years old, as they were once used as a tool of communication and in identifying property.

If you examine a coat of arms, for example, you'll see an arrangement of symbols that may look contrived or silly. I recall examining one aristocratic family's crest and seeing four bees flying amid a red banner, a lion's head, and a golden cup. I thought at the time this was hilarious—why would anyone use bees, such tiny workers, to explain their power and communicate what they stand for? Now that I know what bees symbolize, it makes perfect sense: industry, order, immortality; this is a good promise for the longevity of a clan. The bees complemented the other messages. A red banner was a sign of the blood spilled to preserve their name, the lion's head a symbol of leadership, and the golden cup a symbol of endless abundance.

Of course, this doesn't preclude the use of more obvious symbols, like the lion for pride and leadership, or gold for wealth. Our young country chose stars (hope and brightness) to symbolize each state in a clear, deep field of blue (regality, clarity, and truth).

Symbols are used so often, we often don't even see them. I was impressed when, in the 1996 Olympic Games in Atlanta, the bouquets awarded to the medalists were deeply symbolic:

Olive branch for peace	**Tiger lily** for pride
Laurel for glory	**Two sunflowers** for loyalty
Palm for victory	**Cockscomb** for immortality
Magnolia for perseverance	**Larkspur** for swiftness
Leucothoe for friendship	**Tuberose** for hospitality

You can also choose symbols for your workspace to boost your energies or image, and to send the precise messages to others.

I had a line drawing of an Eskimo warrior in my office when I worked in advertising. My message then was aggressive. I have since shifted my choices to more ancient symbols like shells for enhancing powers of regeneration, a chalice for inexhaustible abundance, and feathers for lightness and air. One creative director at a graphic design firm has a map of the solar system on his wall, a subtle message of his love of exploration and constant drive to "shoot for the stars." Negative symbols are just as telling as positive ones, and should serve as a warning to you. Forget shrunken heads, guns, knives, or other symbols of violence— there's no mistaking their message and they definitely don't attract a positive energy flow.

Knowing the basic language of symbols also helps in reading other people. For example, I try to avoid doing business when I see a horseshoe hung for bad luck (gap side down). I also look for little power symbols as clues to the sensibility of the person behind the desk. Coins are a symbol of abundance, a globe can signify a commitment to intellectual exploration, and a compass is a sign of guidance. When there is no clue to the personality or any symbols per se, it might mean that this person is afraid to express himself.

And just because people have symbols of power in their offices doesn't mean they have the particular power; they may just aspire to it. You'll be able to sense whether their objects are just props or if they have a real attachment to the objects, however. There is nothing more amusing than someone trying to pose as a powerful personality. Keep an eye out for tiresome explanations (trying to prove their knowledge) or for simple detachment as telltale signs.

PSYCHIC POWER SYMBOLS

Acorn	Life
Anchor	Steadfastness
Apple	Wisdom, fertility, love
Arrow	Power
Balances	Justice, impartiality
Beehive	Eloquence
Bones	Life principle
Book	Wisdom
Bow	Willpower
Bowl	Feminine power
Box	Womb
Candle	Light in darkness, illumination
Chalice	Inexhaustible abundance
Circle	Totality
Compass	Unerring, impartial justice
Cornucopia	Abundance
Crown	Victory, dignity, honor
Crystal	Purity, knowledge
Cube	Stability, completion
Dice	Fate, fickleness
Earth	Nourishment
East	Dawn, hope, youth
Egg	Life principle, creation
Elm	Dignity
Evergreens	Immortality, vitality
Eye	Omniscience, intuitive vision
Gargoyle	Ability to scare away evil
Fan	Spirit, dignity
Feather	Truth, lightness, air
Feet	Movement
Fir tree	Boldness, integrity
Flame	Purification, transformation

Fleece	Fat
Fleur de lis	Light and life
Flower	Potential opened
Forest	Realm of the psyche
Fountain	Eternal life
Fruit	Immortality
Garden	Paradise
Gardenia	Feminine grace, subtlety
Gate	Entry, communication
Globe	Eternity, universe
Glove	Honor
Gold	Illumination, wealth
Gourd	Longevity
Grain	Potentiality
Grapes	Wisdom
Grass	Submission, usefulness
Hammer	Masculine force
Hat	Authority
Hazelnut	Feminine wisdom
Helmet	Protection, preservation
Horn	Supernatural power, divinity
Horseshoe (upright)	Good luck
Hourglass	Cycle of life and death
Iris	Hope
Iron	Strength, inflexibility
Ivy	Immortality
Jewels	Hidden treasures of knowledge and truth
Knife	Sacrifice
Ladder	Passing from one place to another
Lake	Magic
Lamp	Wisdom
Lemon	Sharpness
Lily	Purity, birth and death
Lotus	Birth and death

Maize	Abundance
Marigold	Fidelity
Mill	Fate
Mirror	Truth, self-realization
Mistletoe	Life essence
Moon	Feminine power
Mountain	Constancy
Net	Ensnaring, entanglement
Oak	Strength, courage
Oar	Power, skill
Obelisk	Phallic, male power
Orchid	Magnificence
Palm	Righteousness, fame
Peony	Light, glory
Pillar	Connection of heaven and earth
Pine	Uprightness, vitality
Pine cone	Good fortune
Plant	Life force
Rainbow	Different states of consciousness
Rose	Birth and death
Salt	Incorruptibility
Sand	Impermanence
Seed	Latent power, potentiality
Shell	Femininity, life, birth, regeneration
Shield	Protection
Ship	Safety
Spear	Masculine force
Sphere	Perfection
Square	The earth
Star	Divinity
Stone	Stability, durability, reliability
Sword	Protection, authority
Triangle	Heaven, earth, man; or father, mother, child
Unicorn	Purity, incorruptibility

Animals

Animals have been used as symbolic psychic subtexts since man painted in caves. Animals represent power archetypes, and we naturally gravitate to the ones that communicate who we are, be it flattering or not.

Knowing what animal symbols mean can give you insight into yourself and others. Start simply by looking at your domestic pets—if you're a cat person, you're into mystical knowledge; if you're attracted to dogs, you value loyalty and friendship.

Next, consider what kind of animal pictures or symbols you've seen in others' offices. I remember seeing a colorful picture of a parrot (imitation) in a fashion executive's office—probably not the best symbol for her chosen field. Conversely, I noticed one editor at a tabloid newspaper who had a collection of duck figurines (gossip) on his desk, which seemed fitting for his job as a columnist.

Ever wonder why some people collect certain figures? I have a friend who collects otters (happy and clean) and one who collects pigs (fertile and greedy). Do you think NBC knows that the peacock symbolizes immortality and vanity?

Be sure to check out the significance of animal symbols when you visit offices of clients and competitors. You may be clued in to a new dimension of their personalities.

Power Animals

One animal symbol that is very personal, private, and powerful—not just for sending psychic subtext but also for helping you through challenges—is your power animal. These highly individual identities are found through your own psychic access and are with you "in spirit" to help you at your convenience.

I first learned about power animals in the metaphysics class I took while I was still in advertising. The teacher had us sit comfortably, relax, and close our eyes. She took us through a guided meditation, where we (in our mind's eye) walked on a path in any landscape of our choosing. I remember it clearly: I walked along a dirt path on a hill and stopped at the top. The teacher guided us to look around for an animal—she said that one would come to us if we waited. In my vision, I was approached by a mountain lion. After the meditation was over, the teacher explained what each of our animal symbols meant. A mountain lion is quick, fierce, smooth, and a loner. At the time, it seemed to fit. I put a picture of a mountain lion up on my desk at home and, in times of doubt, I accessed its powers to help me find solace and resolution.

I called upon my mountain lion when I was pursuing new business and defending my territory at work. It is remarkable how the animal figure encouraged me to behave in ways I would not have otherwise chosen. My mountain lion taught me the value of stealth in business and the ability to leap upon my target unexpectedly. In almost every situation it worked beautifully.

Native Americans use power animals as sacred archetypes in which each animal has its own "wisdom." Power animals are highly personal and are not meant to be publicly discussed, or they lose their power. I share my mountain lion here because that power animal is no longer appropriate for me—and my current animal companion, who remains with me, is wonderfully effective.

Try to find your power animal with this simple method, and after doing so, look up its symbolic meaning. You may find this animal surprisingly helpful. Use the animal who comes to you for help and advice in situations where you feel stuck or uncertain.

My client Eva's power animal, for example, is a squirrel. At first she didn't know what to do with it—to her a squirrel was just a mild little forest creature who didn't represent any business wisdom she could use. At my encouragement she reexamined the squirrel archetype and realized that she could learn from its quick movements and ability to climb, as well as from its legendary way of storing abundance for times of scarcity. She used her squirrel wisdom to help her garner the positive feedback she deserved but had in the past not used to her advantage. She stored these praises for her annual review—and earned a substantial raise.

Another client shared his power animal, a goat, with me. He saw the goat as a hearty, sturdy companion who could help him scale great heights and walk confidently over rugged terrain. He used his goat during his company's takeover and became, after some uncertainty, head of his division.

Read this brief meditation slowly into a tape recorder, allowing pauses between each sentence—take your time. Play it back to yourself when you can sit comfortably, with your eyes closed.

You are walking along a path. You can see the sky, the ground. Notice what vegetation, if any, grows around you. Walk along, breathing the air, looking at the landscape. Your path takes a turn and you follow it, arriving at a resting place. You stop and look around you. Perhaps you sit down. You sense there is an animal watching you. You relax your breathing, knowing that this animal is a friend. You beckon it toward you, calling softly to it. When your animal arrives, sit with it, let it show you whatever it wants to. When you are ready to leave, thank the animal and tell it that you will respect its powers. Walk back along the path and slowly breathe yourself back into the present.

As with any kind of psychic work, there is a dark side to power animals. Do not encourage any animals who seem malevolent, including vermin, spiders, or snakes with teeth (it's the teeth, not the animal, that indicate evil here; many people find regular spiders and snakes very powerful animals), or any other animal you associate with negative energy or evil. If you do encounter a nasty-looking animal, all you need to do is ask it (politely) to leave, and it will. After all, it's your psychic space, and you have some control over it.

Once you've met your power animal, you may be surprised by what it brings to you. A friend of mine discovered her power animal to be a kangaroo. She figured she'd use it to "hop along" through difficult terrain, but in fact, she found the image of her animal helpful for nurturing some new creative work while she still carried her usual responsibilities. If you get what you perceive to be a friendly little critter, don't worry. You can use even the cutest animals to give you a psychic edge in your work. A squirrel is great for saving up for lean times, and moving swiftly out of harm's way. Don't look at the physical attributes of your animal to see how it can help you out, look to its natural gifts, and call on its instinctual wisdom to lend you some natural psychic prowess.

ANIMAL POWERS

Ant	Industry
Bear	Resurrection, strength, fortitude
Bee	Immortality, order, industry
Bird	Transcendence, imagination
Buffalo	Supernatural power, strength
Butterfly	Immortality, transformation
Cat	Mystical wisdom
Deer	Swiftness
Dog	Loyalty
Dolphin	Worldwide guide, safety, swiftness
Dove	Life spirit, soul, peace

Duck	Superficiality, deceit, chatter
Eagle	Sky gods, the sun, victory
Elephant	Strength, fidelity, memory
Elk/Moose	Supernatural power
Falcon	Victory
Fish	Purification, transformation
Fly	Evil
Fox	Slyness
Frog	Fertility, eroticism
Gazelle	Spirit, liberation
Goat	Superiority
Goose	Longevity
Grasshopper	Improvidence
Hawk	Royalty, nobility
Hen	Procreation
Heron/Stork/Crane	Vigilance, quietness
Horse	Swiftness, reason
Lamb	Innocence, youth
Lizard	Silence
Mouse	Agitation
Otter	Cleanliness, playfulness
Ox	Patience, toil
Parrot	Imitation
Peacock	Immortality, vanity
Pig	Fertility, greed
Ram	Virility
Raven	Prophecy

GATHERING NONTRADITIONAL OFFICE SUPPLIES

I'm sure you're eager to assemble your executive toolbox and set it up for use in your workspace, but take a moment and consider this:

Natural objects can hold both positive and negative powers, so consider their source.

Before you run out and chop a branch off an oak tree for its courage-giving wood, or grab your Aunt Rosie's amethyst from her throat, think twice. Taking objects without respect for their source can result in negativity—a crystal will retain the energy of distress if it is not acquired properly, and could disrupt an atmosphere rather than lend positive vibrations.

The Native Americans always asked the earth to give them what they wanted, whether it was crops, fish, or buffalo, and when they got what they asked for, they said thank you by giving something back. This ritual of acknowledging the earth's gifts is found in most ancient cultures (and used to be more prevalent in our own) and serves as a sort of psychic safety catch so as not to attract times of scarcity or negativity. If you find an object in nature and want to take it with you, leave an offering behind. In a pinch, I leave some hair, but a coin or a stone you've carried is an ideal offering.

When you take a natural object without knowing its history, you could be acquiring a force you'd rather not have. I once picked up a tourmaline crystal from one executive's desk and immediately got a headache; it turned out that he believed it helped absorb his anger and frustration and always held it when under stress. I had no business touching his crystal—but I was seduced by its beauty. Luckily, I had some sage and rosemary with me, and after a quick whiff of each herb I felt better.

I've seen and felt dark energy from many different things, even old glass, pots, and metals. Even when you buy something new, like a set of tumbled stones or a figurine, it could hold energy you just don't need.

CLEARING

As a rule, always clear any power object before you put it in your workspace, and acknowledge it as a gift from the earth. This way you can be sure it will manifest its intended power, and you will avoid psychic hangovers. I've seen one perfectly beautiful piece of quartz crystal completely destroy the atmosphere of an office. Its owner, a lawyer, had purchased it from an art gallery, where she had not bothered to inquire about its origins. After I had been to her offices and noted that it emanated a brittle, tense energy, she called the gallery. She was told that the crystal had actually come from an estate that had to be sold off because of a probate feud. She cleared it soon after and the atmosphere in her office became more open to peaceful and intellectual pursuits.

All crystals and many rocks, woods, and metals can act like a sponge—holding the imprint of an atmosphere until it is cleared of it.

You might as well go out and purchase a big, fat smudge stick right now, because you'll be using it a lot. A smudge stick is a bundle of dried sage, sometimes mixed with sweetgrass or cedar. Smudge, as it is referred to in Native American cultures, is a way of clearing negative energy from an object, a room, or a person.

Light the end of a smudge stick and blow out the flame. The embers create a powerful smoke that will clear negative energies away. The addition of cedar or sweetgrass will create a somewhat softer scent but will still do the trick.

Smudge sticks can be found in natural food stores, bath shops, and many New Age stores. They don't cost much more than five dollars and should last quite a while.

If you can't do the smudge technique, you can soak a power object in salt water and let it stand in the sun for a day. This will cleanse any toxic vibes from it.

REVVING UP YOUR PSYCHIC TOOLS

Now that you have a handle on what nontraditional office supplies are, you are on the verge of becoming more psychically
attuned and more powerful in your business life.

Take your time in collecting your symbols and power
objects, and don't be afraid to change them until you find the
right mix. I mix my objects up at least once every season. By
doing that, you can adjust your objects to your needs, keep your
power fresh, and change the messages as necessary.

THE PSYCHIC POWER OFFICE

Take a little walk in your mind.

You are walking into the office of the president of a company you really want to work for. As you walk in, you notice a
colorful carpet (although not one you'd have chosen). A wooden
table with coffee-mug stains sits in front of a green sofa. There
are paintings on the walls, and plants on either side of a large,
old mahogany desk. The phone is hidden from view, underneath
a mess of papers. There are old books strewn about, a globe in a
corner, and a watering can perched on a side table. How do you
feel?

You have another interview for an equally desirable job at a
different company. As you enter the office of the CEO there,
you take note of this decor: white walls, black leather couch,
glass coffee table with annual reports piled neatly upon it. A single framed print commemorating a museum show of modern art
is on the wall, and the floor-to-ceiling windows are framed only
by unused vertical blinds. The pristine, glass-topped desk is
encased in shiny black metal. The floor is covered with simple
neutral-tone carpeting. There is a bronze sculpture of a nude on
a pedestal in the corner. How do you feel?

Can you tell which office holds more psychic power? And
do you know why? If, in the first office scenario, you felt com-

fortable with the more "lived in" quality of the decor, it did its job and opened up your psychic power centers, making you feel relaxed and open to an enjoyable interview experience. If the second office elicited awe and uneasiness in its perfection and lack of personality, it is far less potent.

This is not a lesson in shunning traditional modern office decor, but in recognizing the value of natural objects, color, and personality.

⊗

Power makes people comfortable so that they open up to you—fear or uneasiness makes people defensive, possibly uneasy, and shut down.

⊗

Evaluate your office and workspace and see if they evoke a hospitable atmosphere. If you want to motivate people to do their best, you might want to create a welcoming, productive environment.

Major power offices vary in style. The executive offices at Columbia TriStar motion pictures are mostly unremarkable office suites, but the hall that leads to them is long, spacious, and lined with Greek columns. This hall evokes a sense of power, and certainly impresses the first-time visitor with the psychic subtext of ancient mysteries. The drama of this message seems fitting for moviemakers.

Strikingly different—but equally powerful—are the executive offices of a major Manhattan insurance company. They are also awe inspiring. The all-mahogany paneling that lines the walls up to the twenty-foot ceilings, the huge old silk Oriental carpets, and the oil portraits of early presidents create a library-like atmosphere. The power is old, steady, and quiet. There is no question that visitors react with reverence and respect.

PSYCHIC POWER ANALYSIS: JANET'S OFFICE

In one female executive's office, I found a bunch of psychic power tools just oozing with good energy. Janet is a high-ranking executive at a large media company. Her L-shaped office cleverly hides her messy desk, so that visitors are concentrated in the most psychically powerful area. She holds meetings at her round, marble-topped table, on which there are family photos. On one wall is a mahogany armoire with books, a video cabinet, and personal objects including a crystal bowl, an award for a show she produced, and a miniature oil painting. Along a windowed wall Janet has placed the blooming orchid plant her husband sent her for her birthday, and a wrought-iron bench with a cushion covered in an Oriental floral chintz. A tall bamboo plant stands nearby. Although the colors she has selected correspond with the company's teal carpeting, Janet has chosen deep green as an accent color. Even her artwork, sketches of teacups in gold oil paint, enhance her feminine power and creativity. From all perspectives, Janet's visitors are influenced by her psychic power tools, and Janet feels alive, alert, confident, and secure in her office space.

PSYCHIC ANALYSIS

Marble tabletop: Connotes that ideas can become real
Wood furniture: Is an all-around energy enhancer
Blooming orchid: Adds energy of love and psychic power
Bamboo plant: Brings protection and luck
Family photos: Grounds the purpose of work
Teacups in gold: Represents wealth and abundance
Green: Represents abundance, earthiness

CREATING YOUR PSYCHIC WORKSPACE

PSYCHIC OFFICE ANALYSIS: HENRY'S CUBICLE

Entering Henry's cubicle, the first thing you notice is his gift for kitsch—by that I mean junk. He has an inflatable cow on the floor next to his guest chair. Numerous "Dilbert" and "Far Side" cartoons are pinned to his walls, and there are many little toys on his desk and credenza, ranging from a walking hot dog to a huge piggy cookie jar, which is always filled with candy. He also has a toy basketball hoop set up over his well-positioned waste-basket. His desk is wood veneer and his computer screen flashes a comic strip screen saver. The scattered papers and pens on his desk overwhelm the tiny cactus plant and the snow-scene paper-weight that says "Hello from Reno." There is also a small, dusty, airline-size bottle of tequila and pictures of his wife and kids.

The lack of natural fibers and substances in Henry's space is obvious, but the amount of humor, ease, and personality he has created permeates the otherwise dead atmosphere. Visitors are tempted to play with one or two of the toys, which makes them more relaxed and therefore less imposing or fearful. Henry no doubt benefits from his playground, as his work is respected and reliable. However, he would find it advantageous to gently amplify the power of his office by adding more plants, some crystals or rocks, and certainly a few less plastic toys or objects (wooden toys are fine) could hold the space better. He may find, with a few adjustments, that his overall physical energy would improve and that his need to be distracted would diminish.

PSYCHIC ANALYSIS

Cactus: Shows a resilience to challenging conditions
Family photos: Grounds the purpose of work
Toys: Contributes to playful atmosphere
Paperweight: Adds the element of water, flowing energy

TIPS FOR YOUR PSYCHIC POWER OFFICE

There are many ways to maximize your office with objects and color—but it doesn't stop there. You can also place your furniture in more "auspicious" positions to help maximize your power.

Napoleon was famous for his "power desk," which he placed far from the door of his receiving room. He made his visitors walk down a very long entryway to get to him. Imagine how insecure one must have felt going to one of his meetings! Napoleon put people off guard so that he would always have the upper hand.

Chances are, your workspace doesn't have that much room. However, if you can move your furniture or desk at all, you can maximize your office power.

- Natural light? Don't put your back to it. Daylight gives you excellent vitality.
- Only electric lights? They give off some low-level energy, but don't count on them being helpful. Get outside occasionally for the real benefit of solar power.
- Place your desk in a "commanding" position, facing people who approach you, but not too close to your doorway.
- Don't face other workers directly, if possible, to avoid potential toxicity and psychic distraction.
- Decorate your office equipment with as much nature as possible to help amplify your own natural powers and cut down on harmful energy.
- Don't hide behind machines or clutter. Using a machine as a barrier between you and a visitor can defeat your power altogether. Machines don't invigorate your power, they hide and detract from it. Clutter can happen, but when it is chronic, no matter how good you are at your job, you are giving out a message of being messy and distracted. Try to keep it to a minimum.

If you are intrigued with psychic power enhancements for your home and office, you may find some methods of *geomancy*, optimizing the earth's energy, helpful. The Chinese art of placement, *feng shui*, is growing in popularity for Westerners. This ancient method of maximizing life-force energy uses the four directions, colors, light, and angles made by your furniture to diminish negativity and enhance psychic power. One word of caution: This is a Chinese method, and our Western psyches don't always agree with that culture's symbols. Whereas we have four elements (fire, earth, air, and water) *feng shui* uses five (fire, earth, wood, metal, and water), and some of the other tools also translate differently. For example, black represents both death and career success, making for an interesting connection. Some colors can even disturb your psychic flow, because you are likely to unconsciously read them from a Western perspective.

If you choose to use *feng shui*, make sure it feels right to you. Harry, a power tools user, changed his home office around to accommodate the rules of *feng shui*. He reported that he really felt different, much less stressed, in fact. Going on his good experience, he added the color red to his decor (facing in the correct direction), but he told me he knew instantly that it didn't work. In Chinese culture, "fire red" is the color for fame, fortune, and festivity. Yet Harry said he felt as if he was staring at a red flag for a bull every time he laid eyes on it. He said the color made him feel emotional and defensive. He felt better after taking it down.

If you are uncomfortable with an arrangement, change it. You can (and should) fiddle with the basic rules of power tools until the outcome feels right to you.

❧ 3 ❧

PERSONALIZED POWER TOOLS AND POWER CYCLES

With the basics of your power office complete, you can turn your attention to gaining a better sense of your own personal power. Various techniques will benefit you on the many occasions when you are not in your own environment.

For walking the halls, attending off-site meetings and business events, or even going on business trips, amulets and charms are excellent portable psychic power pieces. You may also be surprised to learn that your wardrobe is a most effective psychic power supporter (or detractor). Learning the simple rules of psychic power dressing can help you influence how people receive you, how well you communicate, and how well you are understood. Believe it or not, specific accents of different colors can enhance your psychic prowess.

Besides describing the physical means to boost your psychic power, this chapter will also help you assess the highs and lows of your personal power cycle. Akin to the cycle of the moon and the seasons of the year, your personal power cycle goes through both active phases and inert times. Once you know what to look for, you can hook up to the natural power cycle within the context of your own cycle, and effectively plot the weeks and months when you will most likely achieve success. This will help you identify the most opportune times for initiating new projects, closing important deals, and launching new products

PORTABLE POWER PIECES: AMULETS AND CHARMS

You can strengthen your power specifically for different occasions by carrying certain power objects with you (amulets) and by making your own blend of tools (charms).

Portability is key. And although you certainly can leave amulets and charms on your desk (where they are still powerful), they are most effective and convenient to carry in your briefcase, your pocket, or your purse. I use a charm I made for attracting success whenever I want to get my own way, and an amulet made of hematite and gold for grounding my energy when I'm nervous. My client Rob kept an amulet in his pocket to steady him during his company's merger. If you're ever in a meeting with someone you consider your competition or someone you're seeking to impress, you can use a charm to amplify your power, your energy, and your gifts. These objects work by simply accentuating your basic powers and allowing you to present your best possible image.

Amulets

Amulets date back to prehistoric societies, in which certain natural objects were believed to be imbued with protective powers. The objects varied, from simple roots and stones to more elaborate (but natural) objects marked with symbols, like the runic glyphs on the shields of Viking warriors.

Most often, an amulet was believed to protect its owner from a specific evil; for example, to ease childbirth or to avoid disease. However, these tools evolved over time, becoming prized for attracting wealth and luck. From Saint Christopher medals to lucky rabbits' feet, this tradition is alive and well in our culture today.

For the practiced power tools user, an amulet offers creative ways to combine imagery, color, and symbol into a custom power piece. To further make the amulet your own, add or etch some symbol or name onto your power object. This way you can endow it with personal energy and direct its purpose. For example, if you come across a particularly nice stone or piece of wood in the woods, you can write your name on it, your astrological sign, or the power you are looking for. I have a jasper egg with my name on it to help me stay grounded and fertile with creativity. You can do this with just about any natural object, and don't worry about writing on it with man-made ink. The ink does not negatively affect the object's natural powers.

One bond trader I know carries an old Kennedy half dollar in a green silk sleeve as his "winning" amulet. He does very well for himself, and friends and competitors alike have been known to attribute his success to Kennedy.

You can identify your own amulets by allowing yourself to be attracted to one. Back in business school, my old friend Misha found himself at a flea market, staring at old World War II medals. He had no rationale as to why he found them so interesting, being a peace-loving graduate student, so he ignored his impulse to buy one. Still, he found himself thinking about the medals the following week, so he went back to the flea market to pick one up. The medal he chose was inexpensive and Misha pinned it to the denim jacket he wore every day. He considered it his amulet for courage and aggression; whenever he found himself needing to go out on a limb, he concentrated on it for added power.

If you happen to find yourself attracted to an object or symbol, pay attention to the feeling it gives you. Old coins often evoke feelings of wealth or adventure. Watch fobs make some people feel elegant. Even sharks' teeth are thought to bring good luck. Let your psychic sense lead you to objects of power that will further enhance your strengths or compensate for your weaknesses.

Charms

A charm differs from an amulet in that you make it yourself, combining ingredients to produce the desired power. You can make charms to attract success, heighten your intuition, add to your clarity of communication, and even bring you patience during trying times or distress.

Making a charm is a personal process whereby you gather several elements and combine them in a small charm bag. The bag you use should be made of natural fiber and be of a color suitable to your intention (remember the psychic meaning of colors from the previous chapter). Cotton is the preferred fabric, because it breathes best. Wool is also good, but it can be bulky and is more in line with protective energy than with attractive energy. Silk has been used since ancient times as a psychic shield and keeps you clear of intrusive energy from other people. A silk charm can protect you from outside negativity, but for the charm to breathe its power, the bag must remain slightly open, and this can be messy, depending on what's inside.

In making a charm, don't go overboard with materials. Add only one or two herbs to a bag, a very small stone or crystal that contributes to the power of the charm, and whatever else you might find appropriate to your cause. I often write down what it is that I want to accomplish on a small piece of paper and put that inside the bag, too. Remember to keep to a single-purpose intention—a charm made to attract success and wealth and increase your charisma will simply amount to a cacophony of messages that won't accomplish much.

Once you have gathered your charm elements, simply put them in the cloth or bag of your choice and tie it up. As you are tying it, say aloud what you wish the charm to carry. Say, "I endow this with perfect clarity," or "This charm brings me strength and courage," or "This bag brings me wealth," and carry it with you. Charms can last a long time, but once you get what you want, throw the charm away. In getting what you want and giving the charm up, you will be returning the elements to nature so that they can be "recycled" for some other purpose.

Disappearing Pocket Pieces

Charms and amulets seldom lose their power but that doesn't mean they can't be lost themselves. If you ever lose a charm before you feel it has worked its magic, you probably aren't ready for what you want. It is not unusual to lose a charm that you've put too much energy into, especially if you're not meant to achieve a certain goal. For instance, a charm that is psychically charged to make a deal may not work if your deal-making skills are not up to par. What this means is that you may need to use tools to increase your psychic power for courage or wisdom before you can take advantage of some real deal-making opportunities. If that's the case, just make a different charm to address the quality you desire.

If the object is lost and you've achieved your goal, don't see it as a bad sign. It simply means that, having done its duty, the charm went on to find its next owner. Sometimes objects just bail out when they're done.

Negative Power Pieces

Our society has a fascination with "cursed" objects, and for good reason. Most objects from the past become imbued with negative energy if they are disturbed. For instance, an amulet made to protect the tomb of a king will bring bad luck to someone else who carries it. But rarely will you find an amulet made negative just for the purposes of bringing evil upon you. Rather, it's often not meant to be yours.

If you come across this kind of pocket piece, however, it can make your life very unpleasant. You'll know if your object harbors negativity when you find yourself in a bad mood, ill, sleepless, or feeling generally cursed. The best thing to do with a cursed object is to return it to its place of origin. If that's impossible, bury it or throw it into the sea. The earth and ocean can absorb the object's negativity without causing harm to anyone or anything. Just don't give it to someone you like.

AMULETS

Old lockets, necklaces, bracelets or rings, medals, cuff links, tie clips, and chains can be worn to give you support or luck. Amulets are often given to you by relatives or as gifts; when they are personally meaningful they carry psychic power.

Additionally, lots of things you may come across at antiques stores, flea markets, or even in your junk drawers at home can become powerful amulets when they evoke a significant "gut" reaction from you. Any object qualifies as an amulet when it energizes you in a positive way.

CHARMS

Here are some sample charms. Use your own intuition to help you create even more.

Calm: A purple bag of soft wool with a small piece of jasper, bay leaf, and some lavender

Clarity: A blue cotton bag with mustard seed, rosemary, and a small blue topaz or peridot

Confidence: An orange cotton bag with a garnet, ginger, and lavender

Creativity: A black cotton bag with a moonstone, ginger, and walnut

Intuition: A purple cotton bag with a small moonstone and celery seeds

Luck: A light yellow cotton bag with cinnamon, nutmeg, and a favorite stone

MEETINGS:

Sales: A green cotton bag with almonds, mint, and a dime

Crisis: A white silk bag with lavender, mustard seed, and a grounding stone (agate, jasper, lapis)

Brainstorming: A blue cotton bag with an amethyst, vanilla, and thyme

Presentation: An orange cotton bag with blue topaz or sapphire, nutmeg, and walnuts

Negotiations: A green or blue cotton bag with a diamond, nutmeg, rosemary, and cinnamon.

Prosperity: A small green cotton bag with cinnamon, a dime, and some chamomile

Protection: A small black silk bag with onyx and sage

Success: An orange velvet bag containing a piece of silver, a bay leaf, and a piece of paper with your goal written on it

THE PSYCHIC DRESS CODE

Your personal power is also (literally) colored by what you wear. Considering that objects and symbols carry power, it makes sense for your attire also to say something powerful about you. Although the "dress for success" dictum has faded into business fashion history, consider me your psychic fashion arbiter.

Start by taking an inventory of what you already have in your closet. What fabrics are you wearing? What colors do you favor? Do you have accessories that accent or change the way you look or feel? What do you feel is missing from your life? How does that correspond to what's missing in your wardrobe?

The Power of Fabric

Similar to the way it works for charms, **cotton** allows psychic energy to flow both ways. It is light and breezy, allows for clarity, and is associated with air, which is rational, clear, flowing, and invisible.

Wool is nurturing when soft, but formal and protective when stiff. This is an earthy fabric: sturdy, secure, and practical. You may find you are more serious and not as easygoing and "breezy" as you are in cotton.

Silk is a protective fabric that can shield energy. It can be very sensual and suggestive (not good for most business) but can also be soft and smooth. Silk is like the element of water: emotional, fluid, intuitive, and nonrational. Wearing a silk shirt can protect your heart center and your power center (solar plexus) from taking in negativity, and the color of the fabric can send out a positive message to others. In this respect, silk can act as a one-way mirror.

Rayon, nylon, orlon, and **polyester** (all man-made fabrics) are lacking in psychic energy. To carry a power or a vibration of its own, fabric must be derived from nature. It's okay to wear man-made fabrics—just know that they do not affect your psychic power or aid in communication. You'll have to send your psychic messages with scent, color, or through your power centers.

Velvets, rich damasks, chiffons, and **sheer fabrics** generally have no place in the business world. These are fabrics that beg for touch and sensuality. If you choose these materials for your attire, you are sending mixed messages.

Prints and **patterns** (when they are loud) act as a shield of protection. Mixing more than two colors and/or presenting a very complicated pattern simply confuses your recipient—it's like too many opinions vying for attention.

However, a silk tie with a gentle pattern or color scheme can work well. A banana yellow tie with a small blue repeated pattern signifies success and clarity. A deep red and blue striped tie is commanding, strong, and dignified. Unless it is overpowering, it is not the pattern of the tie but the dominant color that provides the message. "Theme" ties (like Nicole Miller's line) send more whimsical messages. Extremely colorful, geometric designs or patterns the make you dizzy or lose focus when you stare at them are too busy to send any psychic subtext. The silk tie is the male version of a silk blouse; it keeps you protected along the heart and power centers but still allows you to send energy out.

Colors

Of course, the color you wear also makes a significant psychic impression. You'll soon see why blue is the most popular color in business.

Red can be protective. It also arouses passion and anger, and grounds you so that you are alert and in a state of readiness.

Orange is a color that brings out emotional responses. Although it has very strong power to attract success, it is not really for business attire. Wearing orange would be like wearing gold leaf to work: too loud and too focused on yourself. I suggest trying on an orange accessory or undergarment, which will do the job without attracting the attention.

Yellow calls in the powers of the sun and vitality. It can boost your personal energy and give the people around you a warm, positive feeling. Again, don't go too far with yellow; dark yellows send a message of cowardice while very bright yellows yell "Look at me!"

Green opens heart energy, so it can affect your objectivity and discernment. Green is a color of life and abundance (which is why our money is green) but it is not often seen in business situations. I don't suggest using green as a dominant color because it reduces your clarity and can make others see you as less than sharp.

Blue increases clarity and is excellent for any kind of work. Any hue of blue evokes a light, airy power, and more important, a nonthreatening spaciousness. It is hard to miss with blue.

Purple opens the door to creativity and spirituality. It is excellent for those of you who constantly need inspiration and imagination. However, if you want to present a more solid and firm image, stay away from purple.

White is a spiritual and ritualistic color that we associate with purity. White does not send a strong message on its own, so it is a safe color for shirts.

Black is the color of mystery and is very popular today. Black shields you from being "psychically read" but also acts as a blank screen so that others can project whatever they want onto you. I see this with women who, dressed in black, look good but unapproachable. It is a good idea to use other methods to communicate your power (with fabric, jewelry, or scent) if you choose to go all black.

Beyond the color spectrum, consider color families.

Neutrals don't send a strong message (that's why they are neutral).

Jewel tones are pleasant but slightly unapproachable.

Earth tones are connected with basic, practical energy.

Pastels are babyish or icy, depending on your attitude.

A note to fashion followers: Interestingly, designers hardly give a thought to power colors and fabrics when they're designing their wardrobes. You need not be overly concerned with color on a daily basis, but when you really want to make a lasting impression, choose your clothing with your psychic eye on the effect. It works.

My own life is a case in point. When still in advertising, I dressed to ask my boss for a raise. The situation merited some consideration: My review was overdue, I didn't like the "big boss" who was in charge of approving raises, and I had definitely earned a reward for bringing in new business and keeping clients happy. At that time, I was not yet well versed in psychic power tools but was fortunate enough to know someone more experienced who was.

She advised me to go with a feminine power suit and to select a fabric that did not send threatening or mixed messages. It was summertime, so I opted for a bright red cotton suit—not too tailored, as that wasn't my style. I chose simple pearl earrings, and underneath, wore a slip of pale pink to add a softness to my commanding red. I slipped a pouch of money-drawing herbs into my pocket.

The suit I chose served several purposes. I looked sophisticated, at ease with my power, and relaxed. I felt good, in command, and optimistic.

Our meeting was very short and most successful. After I laid out my achievements, the boss agreed with me, and after making a show of consulting his budget and keeping me in momentary suspense, granted me the raise I had proposed.

Pay attention to what your clothing is saying, particularly on important days. When you're a woman in a man's world, you don't have to give up your femininity to be heard, but you might not want to send a message of sensual mystery, either. Try to project confidence, security, and power with a pantsuit, soft skirt, or dress. Save the peekaboos and chiffons for leisure-time pursuits.

Power Wardrobe Selections

Here are some tried-and-true power combinations, but these are not the last word on what you can wear. Select what makes you feel your best, with the powers of fabrics and colors in mind. Don't forget to carry a charm or amulet with you to help underscore your psychic power message.

FOR CREATIVITY Women: Soft purples or reds in cotton. You don't have to wear a suit.

Men: Relaxed suit in cotton, blue or neutral tone with a cotton shirt of pink, yellow, or blue, and a tie to complement the shirt—choose a vibrant color or pattern of colors that is not an "everyday" selection.

FOR CRISIS MEETINGS OR PROBLEMS Women: A red, coral, or pink silk suit with black silk shell.

Men: A gray or neutral wool suit, white shirt with dark blue silk tie.

FOR INTELLECTUAL SHARPNESS Women: Cotton or wool blue outfit with white blouse.

Men: Blue cotton or wool suit, blue or white shirt, with blue and yellow tie.

FOR A JOB INTERVIEW Women: Soft wool or silk suit, in blue for rational impressions, soft purple for creative energy, red for making a passionate impression and for protection, if you think you'll need it.

Men: Blue wool or cotton suit with yellow or blue striped shirt, yellow or red tie.

FOR A MEETING TO DISCUSS YOUR FUTURE Women: A combination of soft wool or cotton is most effective. Choose from yellow, blue, or red—no black or neutrals unless you want to be perceived as a blank slate. Choose a suit if it shows an appropriate respect for authority.

FOR POWER MEETINGS AND PRESENTATIONS Women: Try a red, coral, or yellow suit in wool.

Men: Deep blue wool suit, white or blue shirt, with bright red tie.

FOR NEGOTIATIONS Women: Deep blue or purple wool or cotton suit.

Men: Deep blue or gray suit—cotton or wool—white shirt with silver tie.

FOR ASKING FOR A PROMOTION OR RAISE Women: A "power suit" of coral or red silk.

Men: A blue cotton or wool suit with white shirt and yellow tie.

FOR A COMPANY PARTY Women: Wear whatever you like to informal gatherings, unless you're anxious about it; then choose red silk. If you want to do a little politicking, choose blue cotton. Patterns and prints are useful to keep yourself safe from unwanted advances, and black is always right when you don't want to give too much away.

Men: Stay with the standard khaki or chino cotton trousers if it is informal. Consider a sport shirt in nonbusiness colors to give you a relaxed air, like pink, orange, green, or purple. If the affair is formal, a navy suit, white shirt, and red tie are classic and elegant.

YOUR PERSONAL POWER CYCLES

Beyond your wardrobe and the number of power objects you carry with you, your psychic power is also affected by your personal power cycle. This cycle is a product of nature's cycles, moon cycles, and your own birthday cycle. Once you understand the cycles and how they influence you, you'll have greater insight into the times when you should most aggressively pursue your goals, when you're in a more creative time or in "hunter-gatherer" mode, and even when it's best to take some time off. You can work with the natural tide of your psychic energy to align your success rises with natural currents.

Nature's Business Cycles

As you know by now, nature plays a great part in generating psychic power. The more natural substances you have around you, the more alive your space is, and the more psychically powered up you can be.

Nature's cycles also make a profound impression on our psychic energy. Unfortunately, most of us don't notice the natural rhythms of each month because we live in such artificially controlled environments. Our homes rarely match the temperature of the outdoors, and we have the ability to move through intense weather as if it were just a silly nuisance. Even if you do live in a place where you don't have to use heat or air conditioning much, you might just be too distracted to see what our ancestors did: the benefit of the natural prosperity cycles brought to us by the seasons and the moon.

Moon Cycles

I do much of my work by the cycle of the moon and find that it makes me remarkably more productive.

Gauging the moon's cycle, about twenty-eight days, is an excellent way to plan active and less active times. It's pretty simple, too.

As the moon grows from new to full, it gains in size and light. This is a metaphor for gaining energy and expanding—a good time to initiate or carry out new or existing ventures in the outside world.

When the moon shrinks in the sky from full to new, its light slowly disappears. This is the phase of more internal energy, a better time to go over things inside, brainstorm new ideas, tend to existing matters. The waning moon, as it is called, is not a time to excel in the outer world.

This may come as bad news to you. Most of us work in some situation of service, where we don't have the luxury to stay away from new projects every two weeks. (I dare say you wouldn't do well if you declined a new piece of business on account of the waning moon.) That's not what I'm suggesting; you can, however, use moon cycles as guidelines. If you have the luxury of choosing when to initiate a project, choose the new moon, or waxing moon. If you can't wait for that, use your psychic power tools to add to the energy of your initiation. You'll need it to counter the naturally declining energy of a waning moon, which is better for completion than for initiation.

I am so in tune with the moon's cycle that I can feel it start to slow me down in its third quarter (the darkest time, just before the new moon). Even if I try to work against the moon cycles, I find that I can't. The energy just isn't there.

Here are some typical work situations that relate best to either the waning or waxing moon.

Waning Moon (Full to New)	Waxing Moon (New to Full)
Completing established tasks	Starting a new project
Paying bills	Opening a new account
Selling	Buying
Firing people	Hiring people
Leaving a job	Starting a job
Filing	Pitching new ideas
Doing paperwork	Having outside meetings
Focusing on creativity, conjuring ideas	Focusing on initiation, making ideas reality

Considering what went on during the last waxing moon	Using the wisdom derived from the last waning moon
Finishing a project	Signing a contract
Closing a deal	Launching a new product

The moon cycle is a circle of completion, which is why the waning moon complements and feeds the waxing moon. Both are necessary energies (even though most busy people prefer the more active energy of the waxing moon), so try not to resist either, even if you'd rather be out and about instead of doing your paperwork. You need both in order to strike an even balance in your work.

Most of my clients have started using the moon cycles to initiate new work—I constantly get calls asking when the next new moon is so that their precious new venture can be born on the right psychic current. You can find the moon cycles in your local paper, where the weather and tides are reported. The new moon is usually depicted by a black circle (because the sun's light is not reflected on a new moon) and the full moon is a just a circle, indicating full illumination.

Watch your own energy levels during the moon's cycle and see where you're most comfortable. You may even find that your affinity to the moon's phases shifts with the seasons. For example, I am more productive during a waning moon in the winter months, while the reverse is true in the summer.

The Seasons of Psychic Power

Beyond the lunar cycle, we can look to a grander scale of energy around us: the seasons. All the seasons have their own flavor and current, which create a broader psychic backdrop. There is even an emotion associated with each time of the year.

It is necessary to go back in time to truly understand the cycles of the year. Until the advent of technology, societies lived by crop years, tied to the seasons. Our ancestors were naturally attuned to the psychic energy of each season.

Let's start at the beginning: spring. At the equinox on March 21, daylight and darkness are in balance; the sun is directly over the equator. Light is growing stronger in the northern hemisphere, like the new moon growing to full. This is nature's time of initiation. Prepare the ground and plant what you want to grow. The spring is an excellent time to start new projects or ventures. You will be naturally supported by the energy of nature.

The emotion of spring is anger. You're probably thinking, "How could that be? It's such a happy time."

Of course it's a happy time, but like an infant, this newborn cycle comes out kicking and screaming. The energy of initiation is passionate.

SPRING POWER SURGE

On or around March 21:
Light a white candle.
Put some spring flowers in a vase beside the candle.
Write a list of all you want to accomplish by Christmas.
Read the list out loud.
Aloud, ask that all of nature's power support your goals for the greater good.
Blow out the candle.
Keep the list in your office.

Starting officially on June 22, summer begins with the longest day of the year. Summer actually introduces the decline of daylight; every day after the solstice, we lose daylight minutes. It is harder to work in the summer because it is a fallow time: it's too late to plant, too soon to reap. There's not much to do except water the crops, weed, and defend against insects, rodents, or drought. If you want some nonagricultural proof, check out the real estate market. Come March, there is a flurry of home sales and moves; the market picks up. After June, there's a lull until the fall.

Even if it is "business as usual," the summer is a slower time for most businesses. People take their vacations and the heat naturally slows down our desire to be active.

The psychic lull of nature puts us more in the mood to plunge into a lake or laze in a hammock. The natural rhythm of summer is a slow beat, like its opposite, winter; yet we're not compelled to stay indoors. Instead, we are gently lulled into resting and enjoying nature after a hard push in the spring.

Obviously, you can't stop working altogether just because it's summer. However, you do need to be aware of how the season can work against you. Don't expect to have the energy to handle a large workload. Don't try to beat due dates for projects, and do not stress if work is slow. Pay attention to your resistance. You may find yourself getting angry when things don't stick to your schedule, but like plants, most projects take their own time to come to fruition.

If you really need to gear up energy for something, use the waxing moon cycle to help you, and try not to schedule too much when the moon is waning. You'll just exhaust yourself and things won't be all that more productive.

Joy is the emotion linked with the summertime. It is a pleasant fallow time, one that encourages you to enjoy yourself in its long warm days.

SUMMER STAYING POWER

On or around June 22:

Eat dinner outside.

Offer a toast to the season of warmth and joy.

Aloud, ask that natural forces nurture your spring's toil and that the season of rest and relaxation be blessed for you and your family.

Autumnal energy is more active, as I'm sure you've noticed. As soon as cooler breezes blow away summer's heat, you'll find both your energy and your business perking up. By August, there's already a change in the quality of sunlight, and the days are growing markedly shorter. Like the leaves that start to show signs of turning color, our psychic power responds to the shift in the season and prepares to get back to hard work. Remember going back to school? With the arrival of September, everyone became more alert and buckled down to work. Summer officially gives way to fall at the equinox occurring around September 23.

The harvest energy of autumn is very active and productive. Like spring, it's a time to work, although, instead of planting, it's more common to reap what you have sown. This energy lasts until Christmas.

Autumn's emotional flavor is grief, like the end of a party. Even the joy of the harvest gives way to sadness: Work is done, whether or not the harvest was good, the opportunity is over.

HARVESTING POWER

On or around September 23:

Bring out your spring equinox list.

Light a yellow candle.

Place some grapes next to the candle.

Read the list out loud.

Aloud, ask that nature's power help you to harvest the
    goals you planted last spring, for the greater good.

Blow out the candle when you are done.

With the winter solstice on December 22, winter is upon us. This solstice is the shortest day of the year, and the beginning of another fallow time, less comfortable than summer.

Post-Christmas letdown and midwinter blues are all common to the stillness of winter. Daylight is short, provides little warmth, and the light is whiter, almost harsher than summer light. Even in warm climates, trees lose their leaves as if mourning for lost daylight. Although a new calendar year is born, physical energy is low; the ground lies fallow, and most of us just want to curl up and hibernate like bears. The fact that this is a dark time means that it is an internal time, one best used for amplifying your psychic power. It is an auspicious time to reflect on the past year or two, clear out old files to make room for new business, and imagine where you want your business to be in five years. Once you've made room for potential in your files, winter is the best season for brainstorming sessions to generate new goals, products, and business.

Your inclination to "lie low" in winter is natural and normal. The ancients associated this dark time with fear—worrying about whether the harvest would last and if illness or epidemic would take hold. Winter is not a joyful fallow time like summer.

During the imposed stillness of winter, ancient cultures would psychically create the next year and release the old one.

WINTER'S PSYCHIC SOLITUDE

On or around December 22:

Light a white candle.

Place some holly or evergreen beside the candle.

Take out your list from the spring equinox.

Cross out those projects that have manifested.

Write down remaining projects on a fresh piece of paper and add any new things you want to create.

Burn the first list.

Give thanks for what has manifested.

Aloud, ask that your goals be supported by nature during this fallow time and ask nature to feed your psychic power and creativity.

Blow out the candle.

THE PSYCHIC QUALITY OF SEASONS

SEASON	BEGINNING DATE	ENERGY	EMOTION
Spring Equinox	March 21	Active growth	Productive anger
Summer Solstice	June 22	Passive growth	Fallow joy
Autumn Equinox	September 23	Active harvest	Productive grief
Winter Solstice	December 22	Passive harvest	Fallow fear

PLOTTING PERSONAL CYCLES

Do you see a pattern here? Both the moon and the seasons make a cycle of completion. There is a period of growth, like the waxing moon or spring and summer, then a period of decline, like the waning moon and autumn and winter. You can use this model to plot your own cycles.

There are two ways to look at your own cycle. The first uses your birthday as the beginning focal point, the second would use your experience over the last three years to plot out your cycle.

Birthday cycles are easy. First, consider your birthday the spring equinox. For example, my friend Julia's birthday is July 29. She would be in a strongly productive period for the first three months after her birthday, or until October 29. As an illustrator, her business is often slower in the summer and she generally gives herself August, so she doesn't push against the natural current. In September, however, Julia gets to work with a vengeance and tends to have an enormously productive and prosperous period—she once made her entire year's income by November 1.

The second three months indicate a passively productive time. Sometimes she works hard through November, but by December her work is slow and she uses the time to take clients out for holiday lunches. She uses early January to update her brochure and organize her files. The next three-month marker falls on January 29, when a period of active harvesting commences. This indicates a time of achievement and prosperity, perhaps the completion of a project. Julia's work often does pick up during this period and she helps it along by making calls, sending out a mailer, and "hustling" for business. Finally, from April 29 until her birthday, another fallow time occurs, rendering her less likely to want to work or be productive. She tells me that she still works a great deal during this time, but that she gets progressively more tired and stressed as her birthday nears—she is working against the current of her cycle.

To use this method of calculating your personal cycle, just divide the year up into three-month increments starting at your birthday. Each "season" has a subtle shift of psychic energy that, if you pay attention to it, can help you make sense of certain patterns in your business and life and can help you take advantage of these periods of peak performance.

Julia uses her personal cycles more and more to know when to push for her work (in the first and third three-month intervals), or, if she doesn't have the luxury of making her own schedule, to rest more during her low-energy periods, particularly in the fourth month and tenth month of her yearly cycle.

You can use this information to benefit from knowing when to make the most of your energy and when not to push too hard. Generally, in your more productive, energetic periods, push your energy out into the world, as in looking for a new job, getting new business, or launching new programs. During your personal fallow periods, it's a good time to review the past, clean out old files, or catch up on accounting. You'll find that your creativity is sharp—so allow some quiet time in order to access new ideas, visions, and goals.

If your personal cycle is out of line with the natural seasons of the year, like Julia's, look back over your past three years. Note when you had active and productive periods, and when you were more tired or needed a vacation. Your most recent cycles will give you a clue to how the pull of the seasons and your personal cycle work together. Make use of your personal cycle by planning ahead of time, and try to allow your business activities to occasionally correspond with your psychic moods.

It wouldn't be prudent to take a full three-month furlough when you're in a fallow period—you just have to know that your overall energy is low, that you should conserve it and use it wisely. This part of the cycle is the regenerative time, a natural rest period after hard work. When Julia pushed for work in her fallow period, she used to get sick and almost always had a miserable cold at Christmas. Now she takes steps to ensure that she doesn't overextend herself at that time of year.

I often see my clients fighting their natural inclination to take it easy. They think there's something wrong with them when they don't always feel "bright-eyed and bushy-tailed." When I help them work out their personal cycles, they relax. Having an understanding of natural cycles takes the pressure off of having to be "on" all the time—and if you live by the eternal working energy clock of 24/7/365, you'll be losing a lot of valuable psychic power time, and possibly end up with less to show for your work.

Date	Energy for Next Three Months
Your birthday	Productive
Three months later	Fallow
Your half birthday	Productive
Three months later	Fallow

Personalized Power Days

The final note regarding your personal power cycles has to do with two auspicious dates in the calendar year. There is one new moon and one full moon in each year that occur in your astrological sign. The full moon for your sign is the full moon that occurs when the sun is in your opposite sign. The new moon for your sign happens while the sun is in your sign.

When the moon is new in your sign, there is a strong psychic undercurrent for manifesting your wishes. It is like a spring equinox, the beginning of a psychic growth period. The new moon is for wishing for things to come, and the full moon is for releasing what is no longer necessary.

Although there is a natural resistance in our culture to releasing anything, the full moon in your astrological sign gives you the opportunity to diminish problems, disengage from anxiety, and generally rid yourself of any nuisances. It can be very handy, and comes just at the point when you are entering a second productive cycle (usually around six months after your birthday). It is a great time to rid your workspace of physical clutter and clear any obstacles from your path to success.

The Sun Is In		Sign of Full Moon	Sign of New Moon
Aries	(3/21–4/19)	Libra	Aries
Taurus	(4/20–5/20)	Scorpio	Taurus
Gemini	(5/21–6/21)	Sagittarius	Gemini
Cancer	(6/22–7/22)	Capricorn	Cancer
Leo	(7/23–8/22)	Aquarius	Leo
Virgo	(8/23–9/22)	Pisces	Virgo
Libra	(9/23–10/23)	Aries	Libra
Scorpio	(10/24–11/21)	Taurus	Scorpio
Sagittarius	(11/22–12/21)	Gemini	Sagittarius
Capricorn	(12/22–1/19)	Cancer	Capricorn
Aquarius	(1/20–2/18)	Leo	Aquarius
Pisces	(2/19–3/20)	Virgo	Pisces

All you need to do to locate these dates is look in your local paper and determine when the moon is new around your birthday, and when the moon is full around the six-month point after your birthday.

NEW MOON POWER DAY

After sunset:
Light a candle in your favorite color.
Place a plant or your favorite flowers next to the candle.
Aloud, ask that nature's forces join with you in this new cycle of power and prosperity.
Let the candle burn as long as you like.

FULL MOON POWER DAY

After sunset:
Light a white candle.
Place a bowl of water next to the candle.
Aloud, ask that any obstacles on your path be gently removed so that your power can be used to its fullest extent.
Wash your hands in the water.
Blow out the candle.
Throw the water out.

Although these rituals of observance may seem simple or silly to some, they act powerfully with your psychic energy. While you say the words aloud, you shift your own energy, your own unconscious, and allow yourself to access power greater than your own. This is just like the power of affirmations and the power of prayer. This power is to be respected and revered, and you will know no bounds to its effects. Try to get past any resistance you may have—the rewards, both to your spirit and your business, are really very gratifying.

❧ 4 ❧

PSYCHIC POWER
AT WORK

General Practices

Having established an excellent basic understanding of your own psychic power tools and cycles, you can now start to use them consciously in your everyday work life. From the minute you walk in the door, your power centers are humming, your charms or amulets are working to make things go your way, and your office is a stronghold of psychic support. But there's a lot more you can be doing to increase the effectiveness of your psychic power. Let's look at how you could use your new skills throughout a busy workday.

I asked my client Bob to keep a log of how he uses his power tools during an average day. A copywriter at an advertising agency in New York, Bob consulted with me for help in getting from a middle-level position to that of senior writer. See how often he uses his power tools and consider how their applicability might benefit you.

Bob's Log (excerpt)

- **9:00 A.M.** I arrive at the advertising agency right on time and my boss, waiting in my doorway, is asking my opinion about a new project before I can even get my coat off. To avoid getting flustered, I open my power center so I feel confident, and I use my third eye to better "see" something about the project. I surprise myself with an astute observation (this is before coffee!) and I head to my desk.

- **9:15 A.M.** I can't find my assistant anywhere and I need to know if my presentation boards are ready. (I'm presenting my work to a new client and it's a big meeting.) I breathe deeply and send him a little message through my third eye center to get his butt in my office pronto. I run into Toxic Man (the nasty guy in the next office who always corners me to complain about work) and give him sixty seconds of my time while I cover my solar plexus (for protection from his negativity) with my arm.

- **9:17 A.M.** My phone rings and I run to get it. It's my mother and I have to breathe deeply again, this time through my heart center, 'cause I'm really too preoccupied with the presentation to talk to her. I fiddle with the lavender sitting in a bowl on my credenza. A whiff of it calms me momentarily, distracting me from my impatience.

- **9:25 A.M.** My assistant, Gary, appears with coffee and presentation boards in hand. I use the excuse to get my mother off the phone. Gary stays with me as we check the boards for errors. Again I use my third eye. I notice there's a "the" missing in a sentence. Gary leaves to have it inserted. I can tell I'm getting nervous, as my stomach flutters whenever I glance at the clock. I place my feet flat on the ground and concentrate on bringing grounding energy into my body.

- **9:45 A.M.** I head to an agencywide meeting about our new health benefit plan. I use the time to meditate (because the speaker was imparting such trance-inducing energy) and surreptitiously ground myself by nonchalantly holding my hand on top of my head.

- **10:30 A.M.** Back at my desk, I have three voice mails from three different people reminding me to be in a dress rehearsal for the presentation at 11:00 A.M. The real presentation is scheduled for 1:00 P.M.

  I move some papers around on my desk, aware of the fact that I am not all that productive because I'm anxious about the meeting. I check out the moon cycles in the newspaper (for the second time), reminding myself that the now waxing moon is good for expanding ideas and opportunities.

  I take a piece of lapis lazuli and a charm I made for success to the dress rehearsal and keep them in my pocket. I am chastised for not wearing a tie (it is on my desk) but I am complimented on my presentation. I notice that the president of the agency is wearing a blue cotton suit and a yellow tie with blue dots, and I wonder if he's using power tools, too.

  The president of the agency sits next to me during the rehearsal critique and asks my opinion about the marketing strategy. I clutch my charm and speak without hesitation. I consider it successful because my opinion sparked a discussion.

- **12:30 P.M.** I go back to my office to fetch my tie and prepare for the meeting. My tie is a deep blue silk, chosen to give me good communications skills and protect my energy centers from too much toxicity if the meeting doesn't go well. I also sit for a moment at my desk to try to gather my energy so that I'm able to "read" the reactions to my work and respond accordingly.

- **1:00 P.M.** The meeting starts and I'm holding my charm inside my pocket. My hands are sweaty by the time I have to stand and present my boards.

- **2:30 P.M.** The meeting goes great. I know this because I really felt so great in there; I really had everyone's attention—I cracked a few jokes and one of the new clients laughed and joked back at me.

- **3:00 P.M.** I feel exhausted from the day, and I'm finding it hard to concentrate on my regular work. I decide to leave the office for a little walk, and once outside, I breathe in a little sunlight for a fire amplifier and some fresh air for clarity. Almost instantly I feel better.

- **3:45 P.M.** I return from my walk refreshed. I walk into the office with my third eye open, looking for psychic cues of what is to come. I sense immediately that there is a problem at hand.

- **4:00 P.M.** I get a call from another account—there's a crisis brewing in the beer business (no pun intended) and I have to go to a spur-of-the-moment meeting. I think about taking my tie off but leave it on for protection, grab my charm, and head to another office.

- **7:00 P.M.** The beer meeting was long, but we seemed to have worked out a solution. I didn't feel sucked into the panic and I tried sending energy through my heart to everyone to keep them feeling more positive, but I think I was just too tired to give. Instead, I covered my solar plexus and clutched my power charm when I intervened with my opinion. While I spoke I noticed that my throat center felt tight. I took a breath to open it more. I felt relaxed after I spoke my piece and left the meeting without a tension hangover. Back in my office, I returned my charm to its resting place next to the lavender and headed home.

As you can see from Bob's log, there's a power tool for every occasion and using them is quick, easy, and convenient. Bob told me that he is so accustomed to using his tools by now that it is practically second nature to him. He also has reported that since he's been using psychic power tools, he's sleeping better and is more energetic and less anxious in the morning.

PSYCHIC POWER SURGES

Here are some easy-to-use psychic power exercises you can use to:

- Absorb negativity
- Attract success
- Maximize quality
- Manage time more efficiently
- Dream your problems away
- Amplify the elements to your advantage

Psychic Negativity Absorbers

One of the worst aspects of your workplace—no matter where you work—is the toxicity in its environment. I'm not talking about sick-building syndrome; I'm talking about the fact that most office buildings are a black hole of psychic energy, where the emotional residue of your coworkers, be it anger, frustration, jealousy, apathy, or discontent, can be held in the stagnant atmosphere of artificial materials. As you know, flameproof carpeting, plastics, and electronics and climate control do not feed the energy of your office, nor do they neutralize negativity by absorbing it as some organic materials do. Heavily toxic atmospheres impede productivity and satisfaction.

Toxicity collects in an office environment because it has nowhere else to go. Consider how many people come and go all day and how much anxiety, fatigue, or anger they might be carrying with them. Whatever emotions people bring to work make a lasting psychic imprint on the atmosphere, which is generally not joyful, easy, light, or compassionate to begin with.

The more natural objects and fresh air you can get in your office, the less toxic your atmosphere will be. You can also use power tools to deflect psychic negativity around you.

Negativity Deflectors

- Place an onyx, citrine, or peridot on your desk.
- Smudge your office with sage after hours.
- Sprinkle sea salt along the doorway or entryway to your workspace. This cleanses those who enter your environment.
- Cover your power center (solar plexus) with your arm or some files whenever you are in the presence of someone who is "letting off steam."
- Wear red or silk undershirts for protection.
- Place a decorative mirror on your desk. Most visitors will find it nice to look at and won't realize that it's reflecting their own negative vibes back at them.

Toxicity is very hard to release once it has built up within you. Be sure not to release it all right away, anyway, because cleansing your psychic centers can result in some unpleasant feelings.

Toxicity is caused by the inability to release negative feelings—not short-term frustration or aggravation but prolonged exposure to something you find disagreeable and have no control over. Just feeling generally unhappy and unable to make a difference usually leads to toxicity. People who are very toxic are also very bitter.

I once worked for possibly the most toxic person I ever met. He was a creative director in advertising, a bad drunk, and a screamer. This guy was so toxic that people in my office begged me to slip him something to keep his mood swings to a minimum and spare us his wrath.

I was only a beginner in metaphysical practices at the time, and I wasn't really sure what to give this monster. I chose a watermelon tourmaline, a crystal that helps people transform and shield negativity. I thought perhaps he would mellow out somewhat with this energy, and maybe become a little nicer.

I gave the crystal to the creative director as a present (it was generally known that I was into this stuff, and people were curious about it). He thanked me for it and seemed to settle down for few days.

I had begun to think that the crystal had done its work when I heard a general commotion coming from his office, and a new assistant emerged red-faced and tearful. No, I was wrong—but I didn't know how wrong.

Moments later, the temperamental executive was standing beside my desk, looking down at me. I felt my energy wither, wondering what I was in for.

"Something's really wrong with your crystal," he said.

I looked down at his outstretched hand and saw nothing but sand. I didn't understand. He pointed to it.

"That's what's left of it."

I couldn't believe my eyes and shook my head in disbelief. A few shards remained of the once pretty tourmaline point. He left the dust on my desk and walked away.

When I consulted my teacher about what had happened, she explained that the crystal probably couldn't take the toxicity this guy was giving off, so it crumbled.

I smudged our offices one night after work and gave a small piece of onyx to everyone who wanted it.

More Negativity Deflecting—Fear Releasing

Some people become afraid when they work with their psychic energy because they fear their own power, their own dark side, and what may be unleashed as a result. Others are more open to their power, but are afraid of specific situations—like public speaking, risk-taking, or succeeding (curiously more common than a fear of failure). Generally, most fear manifests itself as negativity—and sometimes the very reaction we fear appears just because we've put so much psychic energy behind it. Fear tends to reveal itself at the most inopportune times, such as when you've actually gotten what want or you get some sort of "proof" that your psychic power tools are really working. After you've worked hard to get what you want—recognition, new opportunities, more power, success—there is always a little psychic kickback where you need to find the courage to accept what you've asked for.

I cannot tell you how many times my clients called to say they finally got what they wanted and weren't so sure they wanted it anymore.

Sue, a management consultant, pitched a new client for the opportunity of restructuring his midpriced women's fashion stores. Sue had relevant expertise in retailing, primarily in upscale, high-end fashion. She wanted this account because she had some very innovative ideas she knew would work well. To acclimate herself with this prospective client, she took appropriate business steps (visiting the stores and their competition, reviewing sale histories, reworking her standard sales presentation to suit the style of this market segment). She also used some psychic power tools to boost her own confidence and impress her prospect. She carefully chose her power wardrobe from his line of clothing, wearing a gold-colored wool suit and a soft yellow scarf. (She cleverly had the suit tailored to fit her like a glove.) Sue also carried a green charm bag containing a small piece of carnelian and some rosemary to bring her keen insight, creativity, and prosperity. Her enthusiastic new approach to his business was helpful in winning the account, but the minute she won it, she wondered why she had gone after it in the first place. In trying to articulate her fear, Sue came to the conclusion that it was a basic fear of failure. What if her psychic powers had "oversold" her?

Sue's dilemma was familiar to me. Any time you stretch yourself and take a risk, there is fear. Psychic power only enhances your power—it won't attract something that you can't do or destroy you (although your fear will do that for you). Sue's powers would not have helped her to succeed in attracting this business if she weren't qualified. Be conscious of your fear—it makes you distrust your instincts and distances you from your power.

•••

Your fear can actually destroy your hard-won gains.

•••

When you are faced with fear, I recommend psychic dissipation. You can use one of two simple methods to confront your fearfulness and get on with your work:

- Breathe through it.
- Burn it.

Breathing through fear is accomplished through your power centers. Because this exercise is like a guided meditation, read the following instructions into a tape recorder and play it back to yourself on your tape player.

EXERCISE FOR
BREATHING THROUGH FEAR

Sit with your feet on the ground or lie down.

Breathe naturally, listening to each breath.

Inhale, exhale.

Slowly, naturally, allowing your breath its natural rhythm . . . (pause) . . . open up to your heart center. Breathe green energy through it as you inhale and exhale (pause). Feel your compassion, your love, your peacefulness. Your heart is soft and hopeful (pause). Gently breathe your heart energy and let yourself be held in its serenity.

Now, moving just beneath the heart, feel your solar plexus. How does it feel?

Is it tight with fear? Numb? Aggressive? Weak? Breathe gentle yellow energy into it. Sunlight is streaming into your diaphragm, inhaling and exhaling sunlight (pause). Your breath is calm, natural. Allow it to find its own rhythm, breathing sunlight in and out (pause).

Now allow yourself to face your fear. What is it? What does it look like? Look at your fear while breathing in the sunlight, keeping your heart center soft.

You are safe in your light. You cannot be harmed.

Gently breathe, looking at your fear.

As you exhale, allow your heart and solar plexus energy to approach the fear. Send yellow and green light toward it.

See your fear dissolving in the light. Watch it become transparent, dissipating into the air. You can even move your entire body through it, your fear is now so light.

You may not want to get close to it, though. And that's okay, too. Just watch it soften, loosen, fade. Your psychic energy is so strong and large that your fear becomes small and weak.

When you no longer feel afraid, or when you feel your fear has faded substantially, close your solar plexus by taking back the yellow light with each inhale.

You may allow your heart center to stay open. Breathe naturally, allowing your psychic energy to return to your body. Find your feet and wiggle them. Rouse yourself back into reality.
Repeat as needed.

After you do this exercise once, you can try it as you go about your day, opening your heart center and solar plexus and breathing light around fear as you feel it come up. Although it won't be as powerful as this meditation, it can help neutralize your fear.

EXERCISE FOR BURNING YOUR FEAR

For this exercise you must be in a place where you can safely burn a piece of paper. I recommend a sink where you can put out a fire if need be.

Write down your fear on a piece of paper. Write as many different kinds of fears or fearful outcomes as you wish. Draw your fear if you can. Use magic markers, crayons, pencils. Allow your most childish impulse to emerge.

When you feel that your fear has been adequately expressed on paper, take it to be burned.

Before setting a match to your paper, surround yourself with white light. Know that your fear cannot penetrate your light barrier.

Set your fear on fire. Allow it to burn thoroughly.

Take the ashes outside to the garbage.

Watch out for psychic kickbacks with this fear releaser. Fire is a very powerful medium for release, but it often encourages your fear to rise to the surface so that you can feel and release it. It is normal to have a little panic attack after you do this exercise.

If by some chance part of your paper does not burn, it is a sign that you are not ready to release all of your fear. Don't worry about it. Just see how this exercise plays out—and give it two weeks before you do it again.

ONE MORE NOTE ON FEAR Not all fear wants or is meant to be released. Sometimes you just have to learn to live with it. And it is unreasonable to expect that you can live without any fear.

Remember to look into your fear closely so that you can identify what it's really about (making money, job security, gaining a reputation, losing a key account) and let it go. Fear provides a message, not a dictate. Don't live your life ruled by it or you won't have any life at all.

Psychic Success Attractors

If you can successfully navigate the negativity in your work life, you are ready to attract success.

In order to open yourself up to success, you do need to be clear (so salt yourself in your shower). It also helps to have a decent handle on your power centers. Try grounding and centering yourself.

If you are so far prepared, it is time to experiment with psychic magnets.

To attract success, use your third eye to visualize what you want, but don't visualize how you get it. Try to see yourself as a psychic magnet for success, and the things you want will be drawn to you as you grow stronger.

Gather your success magnetism by using these methods:

- Keep your power animal active—consult your animal wisdom in meditation.
- Keep your power objects near you.

- Wear success-attracting scents, such as poppy, vanilla, citrus, ginger, cloves.
- Don't be afraid of your own power; release fears periodically.
- Keep your solar plexus open but keep your will (the aggressive part) low.

Quality-Maximizing Techniques

Often you're in a situation where your work is reviewed, critiqued, accepted, or rejected by others. Your psychic work is by no means done when you're ready to put that prospectus in the FedEx envelope or you're sending that memo via interoffice mail. You can psychically charge your work to make it seem more inspired, acceptable, powerful, and/or profitable to others.

There are a number of quality-maximizing techniques to choose from; the key to each is remembering to do it (which is, I know, not easy on a busy day).

- Charge it with energy for success.
- Send your heart energy into the work (close your eyes and concentrate on sending green light from your heart center). Any work sent "from the heart" has a better shot at success.
- Send your power animal along with the work. Note that I mean asking your power animal to "accompany" the work and deliver it with its best energy.
- Allow your power charms or amulets to rest on your work before you send it out. This charges the work with their properties.

One of my clients, a recent college grad, was having a hard time finding a job. He was working as an administrative assistant at an insurance company, and knew it was not going to lead anywhere. What he really wanted to do was get into a software company, but he didn't have the connections or any related experience. The only thing he had going for him was his commitment, drive, and self-taught technical expertise.

He asked me how he could psychically charge his résumé to make it more powerful. Because he was sending his résumé electronically using the Internet, he couldn't use charms or power objects to give his message a boost.

He developed a list of companies he was going to target, and researched them to the best of his abilities. With the information about each company in mind, he devised a customized cover letter for each company that he was also going to E-mail. When I asked him what his E-mail address was, he gave me a rather dull numerical combination that preceded his server's name. Here, I suspected, was an opportunity for a little cyber psychic power. Without too much trouble, he acquired another E-mail address (just for this purpose) based on his power animal and his lucky number, "7jaguars." When he sent each E-mail, he visualized his jaguar cutting through the mounds of E-mail and other résumés each company received and finding the right moment for his résumé to arrive. Of the ten companies he contacted, he received responses from all, and two of them showed real interest. After a lengthy dialogue with the young CEO of one of the companies, he obtained an interview (during which he was able to use his power tools), which led to another interview, a referral, and eventually a job at a small start-up. My client enjoyed the process because it gave him the confidence to attain his goal as well as an understanding of how to use his psychic power tools to stack the intuitive deck in his favor.

Whether you are going for a promotion or need to have a good meeting, you can use your power tools to enhance your likelihood of meeting that goal. However, don't obsess over your goal. You can psychically drown the life out of it, like overwatering a plant, just by wanting it too much. If this happens to you and you don't get what you think you want, it may be because your magnetism can attract a better situation. Keep those psychic knees bent, and be sure to look at success as a multilayered creative experience. Success is a continual and gradually unfolding process. Be sure to define your own success by your happiness, not just by your title, salary, or what other people expect you to have achieved.

Focus-Pocus: A Cure for Distraction and Procrastination, the Adversaries of Success

Being mentally distracted or energetically idle is not only very unproductive—it can also be psychically detrimental. We all fall victim to mental haziness, which occurs when our crown and third eye centers are overloaded. Being unable to focus is a symptom of not being grounded—and when you're not grounded, you're not using your psychic energy consciously. Being out of focus is fine for the hammock, the couches, a walk in nature, or anywhere you don't have to be "on." It's not fine for work.

When we become unfocused we are lacking in the element of earth. To regain focus, you need to ground yourself by closing your crown center and opening your root and navel centers. Use the following exercise to ground yourself whenever you're feeling "out to lunch" or if you're experiencing difficulty concentrating.

EXERCISE TO GROUND

Stand or sit with your feet firmly planted on the ground. Put your hand on the top of your head, on the crown center. Hold it there.

Close your eyes. Visualize the energy coming from the center of the earth and traveling up into your legs through and into your body. Watch it travel all the way up to your crown center.

> *As the energy pulses up, allow it to open each energy center. First the root, then the navel center, then the solar plexus. Stay with the first three centers for a while before you move on to your heart and throat. You do not have to concentrate on the third eye or the crown center because they are overactive.*
>
> *Feel the energy pulsing in your body. When you feel ready, open your eyes and put both of your hands on the floor. This will continue to ground you.*
>
> *Slowly sit up and return to your work. If you still feel spacey, repeat as necessary. You can pat the top of your head every few minutes to keep your crown center closed.*

PSYCHIC TIME MANAGEMENT

I can practically hear you already:

"But I don't have the time to do all this power tool stuff!"

Nonsense. You have all the time you need. You can practice with your psychic power anytime—even in your sleep. Remember how my client Bob's log revealed that he meditated in an agency meeting. I happen to like to meditate at home, but when I'm on the run I use prolonged time on planes, trains, and automobiles in order to stay in touch with my saner side (you have to find some way to survive New York City traffic). When you're waiting for an elevator, waiting for your lunch date, or even waiting for that big meeting to finally begin, you can be honing your power with your power tools, just by squeezing a charm or opening a psychic center.

Although I know that it probably feels that your time is stretched to its breaking point, and you just can't accommodate one more task in the middle of your busy day (even if it is while you're waiting for an elevator), I'm going to change your mind. In fact, I'll change your concept of time altogether.

We mark time deliberately to measure our years, our lives, and to give us a way to understand natural cycles. But time hasn't always been measured like this. Ancient cultures measured time only by the new and full moons to mark the market days during the growing season. When the earth was fallow, no one even bothered to mark time. What a concept—no January, February, or March.

I tell you this so that you know you can have a totally different concept of time, if you want to.

The way to alter time is to employ a psychic practice called time shifting. This technique requires some skill (that means it's not easy) but once you get the hang of it, you'll find it pays off as a stress reliever.

Time shifting is the ability to make time last "longer" when you need it to, and to make time pass more quickly when you can't wait anymore.

Everyone has, at some point, experienced the fact that some time takes just ages to pass, while other times simply fly by. Ask any schoolkid and he'll tell you that the most boring sixty-minute lesson takes at least three days to be over, while the same period for lunch or for taking a test can fly by. It's not just because you're busy—it is its own reality.

I feel the autumn season goes by in less than a blink of my eye, while winter and summer drag on for what feels like six months. My friend Susie says summer is always the shortest season. Everyone has his or her own experience of time, so don't be afraid to work with your psychic power to shift time into a framework you need. You'll be able to meet those once impossible due dates for presentations and you'll find that the pain has been taken out of previously excruciating conferences. All you need is a little psychic power behind you and you can make time meet your preferred pace.

Time Stretching

Sandi, an architect, was concerned about making the Christmas due date for her current project. She was worried because she was running out of time and a lot of events on her calendar prevented her from spending the kind of concentrated energy she needed to get it done.

Sandi decided to use power tools to keep from panicking. She closed the door to her office and lined up her energy centers. Even as her phone rang, she kept herself in a centered and calm state. She eventually calmed her breathing into a meditative trance state, and opened her third eye. She visualized herself completing her project and presenting it to her associates. She even noticed that her visualization included what she was wearing at the time (a deep green suit with a Christmas pin on the lapel), so she knew she was on time. As she held this vision, she inhaled deeply, breathing space between her and the vision. She exhaled into the future, expanding the time between then and now. With each breath, the time between her and her project due date got larger.

Sandi stopped breathing her energy into the future when she felt comfortable with the psychic buffer she had created. She noted that she felt at this point that she had plenty of time to complete the project, but a week later, her anxiety returned. That isn't unusual—the power of shifting time sometimes needs to be refreshed. Time is elastic, stretching and bouncing back to a shorter state, so Sandi repeated the process twice more. She not only completed her project on time, but presented the results with the confidence and panache that came from staying in control of her progress.

To elongate the space between you and a due date, or in other words, stretch time, just do as Sandi did.

EXERCISE FOR STRETCHING TIME

Sit in a quiet room.

Line up your power centers.

Visualize your goal. See it clearly and calmly in your third eye.

Breathe gently, so that you are calm.

Increase the depth of your breath gradually.

As you exhale, breathe into future time, expanding it with each breath.

Breathe into the future until you feel comfortable with its expansion. Use your heart center by breathing energy out of it. Feel the calmness, knowing that there is time enough for everything.

Allow your breathing to return to normal, close your third eye by rubbing it. Slowly return to your everyday consciousness.

Repeat as needed.

Warning: This exercise is not a panacea for procrastinators; it is a way to psychically give yourself enough time to complete your task. You still have to do the work!

Speeding Up Time

Be sure to examine your motives before encouraging time to fly by. Even a painfully long experience often has its merits.

I have a propensity to want to speed time up, which usually ends up causing some sort of dilemma: You may speed up the time it takes to hear back from a prospective client, and then, in retrospect, regret that you didn't take advantage of the downtime you could have had if you waited.

Here's an example: jury duty in New York City. Prior to its reform, the system by which citizens served was the bane of the business world: two weeks of sitting in a large room, waiting to be called to listen to cases you weren't even selected for. Even if you eventually served, those first two weeks were wasted with delayed court times, stalled cases, and hours of jury screening and selection. Needless to say, two weeks is a lot of time to "waste."

This was my first attempt at speeding up time. I was a novice, but I was determined to make my jury service fly by. Instead of watching the clock, and being distracted by other jurors suffering from impatience, I focused on the exercise for speeding up time. I must have done it twice every morning and afternoon for the first two days I was there. Then, quite unexpectedly, on the third day I got called into a case that was settled within moments of the jury briefing—and by midday I was excused.

Back in the chaos of the office I realized I had squandered valuable time in the jury waiting room. Why was I in such a hurry to return to the mess of the office? Now I rarely use the speed-up process, even during a painful time. Speed things up when you must, but don't get in the habit of rushing yourself toward the end of your life.

EXERCISE FOR SPEEDING UP TIME

Wherever you happen to be, find a way to sit still and place your feet on the ground. Close your eyes or look down into your lap. Let your eyes unfocus.

Breathe through each of your centers, starting from the root, moving upward through the navel, solar plexus, heart, throat, third eye, and crown centers. Feel your energy expand as you move up.

Stay with your third eye and crown centers, breathing the purple and white light through them.

In the distance, visualize the end of this time, the point where you want time to be sooner, rather than later. Breathe in this vision, sending your heart energy through each breath. Surround it with your heart energy.

Draw the vision closer to you, as if your heart energy was bringing it back to you. Take your time. Use each breath to bring it closer.

When you feel the time is upon you, that your vision is just in front of you, release your hold on it.

Now as you inhale, breathe your heart energy back into your heart, leaving the vision in front of you.

When you feel complete, close your energy centers, starting with the crown and working down through the third eye, brow, throat, heart, solar plexus, navel, and root. To close each center, inhale the color that corresponds to it.

When you have closed all your centers, open your eyes and/or focus on your surroundings. Place your hands flat on the ground. Feel the earth beneath you and take in its energy.

DREAMING OF PROBLEMS . . . AND SOLUTIONS

Another way to make use of the psychic power of time is to learn to understand your dream time. Dreaming provides you with a psychic landscape you can use easily and effectively to address problems and generate solutions in your business life. You won't want to do this every night, of course, because when you're working with psychic dreams you won't get much rest. However, if you want to run a problem by your subconscious to come up with a possible solution—or you want to know if something is going to work out, you can simply ask yourself to dream about it and see what the dream says.

Of course, there is one small complication to this seemingly easy process: We dream in metaphors. You might ask to dream about the outcome of a new project, one you really want to succeed, and you end up having what seems to be an entirely irrelevant dream. Perhaps you dream that you're pregnant or that you've just had a new baby. That would mean, in metaphorical terms, that you are going get that new project, but you either have to wait for it (pregnancy) or it is still in its early stages (infancy). If the baby wasn't yours—or you found yourself yearning for someone else's baby, the project may go to someone else.

I once asked to dream about a book I wanted to do. At the time, I was also working on a deal to sell film rights to another one of my books. I dreamed that I was pregnant with twins and that I lost the babies. I wasn't upset in my dream, and before waking up I remember deciding to get pregnant again.

Dreams (unfortunately) can be prophetic. My book idea got shelved and my film deal fell flat. However, this coincided with a different, sudden idea for a book that sold quickly.

Dream Interpretation

It can take time to become fluent in the language of dreams so I suggest you pick up one of the many good books available on dream interpretation. To get you started, here are some standard dream symbols and what they mean.

SOME COMMON DREAM SYMBOLS

DREAM SYMBOL	INTERPRETATION
A hospital	A situation that needs mending
A hotel	A temporary transition
A house or building	Your life or body
Office	Hard work, solving a problem
Prison	Restriction
School	Learning about something new

A dark room	No answers yet
A messy room	Problems
A dilapidated room	Something needs your attention
Going upward	Dealing with the outer world
Going downward	Dealing with internal issues
Opening a door or window	Opening to a new experience
Not going through a door	Not facing a problem
A car	You
A road	Your life
Your feces	Making money, abundance
Dirty bathrooms	Dealing with other people's shit
Flying	Freedom, feeling good
Falling	Fear, losing control
Tornadoes	Unpreventable, brief threat
Volcanoes	Anger
Smoke/Steam	Confusion about anger
Being pursued	Anxiety
A crowd of people	The need to make a decision
Dying	Transformation, starting afresh
Having a baby	Starting a new project
Losing a baby	Your project may not be viable
Being naked	Vulnerability
Losing teeth	Self-esteem issues
Animals	(See interpretation in chapter 2)

Bad Dreams

You don't have to wake up sweating to know you've had a bad dream. But you can count yourself lucky, because they are often a way of working out problems and releasing fears in your dream-scape, which is far more desirable than manifesting them in reality.

You often work out your anxieties and fears in your dreams (falling, running, being pursued, being ill, showing up for a meeting unprepared). These dreams may not be pleasant but they are very healthy—they purge you of emotions that are hard to access in your daily routine. Consult the dream symbol chart to make sense of your bad dreams, or if you want to go further, I recommend reading Carl Jung's essays. He interpreted many symbols, and like Freud, used dreams to better understand the human psyche.

How to Use Your Psychic Dreamscape

Just to be safe, don't take your dreams at face value. Even if your dear old grandmother comes to you with prophecies (and this can happen), don't take them too seriously. You are likely to misinterpret even her well-meaning messages.

That said, dreaming for psychic insight is really easy. All you have to do is ask to dream about a certain topic before you go to sleep.

Do not take your dreams literally.

> *In bed, with the lights out, say aloud:*
> *"Tonight I want to dream about how to get that promotion and I want to remember the dream."*
> *or*
> *"Tonight I would like to dream about whether or not the deal with _____ will work out, and I want to remember the dream."*
> *or*
> *"Tonight I want to dream about a new career, and I want to remember the dream and I would like to be able to interpret the dream with ease."*

That's it; simply ask to dream about your subject that night, and ask to remember the dream. If you want to try to make it simple, ask for an easily interpreted dream.

Your psychic power in dreamscape works differently than in physical reality. You're simply not as limited. You can walk through walls (move through obstacles), hang around with monsters (confront threats) and aliens (assimilate to new people), even get killed but survive (undergo transformation). And if the dreams get really weird, don't worry, you're dealing with a totally different realm, one that is a lot safer than the real world.

It is important to recall not only the symbols of your dream but also your feelings in the dream. Were you angry, sad, fearful, happy, cautious? It is important to interpret your dream with emotional information so that you know what symbols mean. Keep a log of your dreams so that you can track your progress.

For instance, when my client Alice was about to start a new job, she asked to dream about her new boss and whether or not they would get along. In her dream there was a dog who followed her around everywhere. She felt that the dog was "sweet" but that she couldn't get rid of him. Upon waking, Alice realized that her dream told her that her new boss would be too "hands on" but loyal and friendly. If the dog had been mean or had shown her his teeth, her dream would have taken on a totally different meaning.

Don't be surprised if many of your dreams are in some way negative. It is easier for us to process problems and to be warned of them in our dreamscape than to deal with them in real life, and our subconscious mind knows this.

If you do have a dream that really disturbs you, and you're having trouble getting over it, go back into it and change it. This is like meditating, done quietly, with your eyes closed, so that you can conjure the dream again. This is a way you can take it further, change how you react, or look for more symbolism to clarify the dream's message.

If you want to go back into a dream, try doing so with a friend or partner listening to you. He or she can act as your guide and ask you questions so that you can accomplish whatever it is you are after.

Use your ever-increasing ability to be still here. All you have to do to get yourself into a quieter state is close your eyes and calm your breathing. Conjure the dream in your third eye, and while watching it, describe it out loud. Recount the dream in the present tense as if it were happening at that moment.

Here's an example. My client Anne was having some difficulty at work and asked to dream about the situation with me as her guide. Her dream:

> I am walking downstairs in a dark and scary place. I open
> a door and hear moaning and crying in a dark room. I
> am afraid . . . the crying won't stop. I don't know what to
> do . . . then I wake up.

With my help, she went back into her dream to get more information and to try to resolve the anxiety and unhappiness she was feeling.

> I don't know what to do. . . . I am afraid, so I reach out
> and feel a switch on the wall. I turn on the lights and see
> a mother crying over a child's sick body. I feel compelled
> to help them. I lead them up the stairs to a better place.
> It is okay.

Anne was having problems with a female boss when she had that dream. She interpreted the message as looking within herself for the solution (going down the stairs) and enlightening herself (turning on the light), as ways of finding peace of mind. She asked for a solution to her problem in her next dream, now that she no longer felt helpless and afraid.

You, too, can heal a problem through a dream and even take action to bring it to some sort of psychic resolution—but you have to remember it first! Try to keep track of the dreams that make an impression on you, and you're likely to find a common theme.

The best dream interpreters are still psychotherapists, so if you have real issues to resolve or simply want to know more about interpretation, pack up your dreams and take them to a professional.

ELEMENTARY POWER AMPS AND DIMMERS

Beyond the dreamscape, we all have our "blah" days or off moments. They are part of life, and most of the time they don't pose life-or-death consequences. But if you happen to be facing an important decision or event on an "off" day, don't leave the fallout to chance. Imagine being off your mark when you're meeting someone who could dramatically influence your future. A bad hair day looks good compared to that feeling.

You can use your psychic power to get you back on track even on the worst day, by using these quick "elemental" fixes. Elemental amplifiers are simple "zaps" for focus and clarity. Dimmers will tone down your energy if one of your elements is out of control.

You may remember from chapter 1 that your power can be broken down into the four elements: fire, earth, air, and water. Each element contributes differently to your overall power, and there are times when you are low on one or two. For instance, your energy could be low, you could feel sluggish, as if you have "no fire in you." That's generally an indication that you could use a little firing up. If you're "low on air" you would be experiencing problems with articulation and expression. You would be spacey or unproductive when you're experiencing an earth-related problem. And your water element is at low tide when you lack fluidity and emotional energy.

Of course, there is the possibility that an element is too strong. Too much fire is expressed by an inability to sit still, or feeling a general sense of anger or aggravation with everything and everybody around you. A "spitfire" is not a very likable or powerful person. Too much earth can make you immobile, dull, or docile, qualities any sharp executive would want to avoid. Too much air causes nervousness and an inability to concentrate, hence the names "airhead" and "windbag." Water can weigh you down with emotion, make you sentimental, and affect your judgment and decision-making skills adversely.

It is neither necessary nor possible to always be in balance. Yet if you're in a situation where you really need to get it together, you don't want to leave balance to chance. Try these elemental power boosts. You can take a few minutes to cover each element, or you can simply home in on the element you need to fix.

Follow the instructions for elemental amplification if you are deficient and if you need to tone things down a bit, follow the steps for elemental dimmers.

FIRE AMPLIFIER Light a match or a candle. Look at the flame, from its blue end to the tip. Breathe in the power of the flame (not the flame itself—this is not a circus act). Imagine the flame going into your body through your breath, and into your blood, your bones, your muscles. Feel the heat and the light. Feel your passion return to you.

Stare at the candle for sixty seconds. If you're using matches, it will probably take a few matches to make it to a minute, but it's worth it.

FIRE DIMMER Look into a wastebasket. Open your power center. Imagine fire coming from your solar plexus and into the wastebasket. Nothing catches fire, of course, but you know that your excess fire energy is being emptied into this place. You don't even feel your body as you release this excess energy. Keep the vision going for sixty seconds. Notice how calm you become.

EARTH AMPLIFIER Place your feet firmly on the ground and imagine the earth's vibrations coming up from the center of the earth, through the foundations of your building, into the flooring, up the walls, and into your feet and body. See the earth's pulse vibrating through your body. Feel its comfort and sturdiness. Hold for sixty seconds.

EARTH DIMMER Sit down and take your feet off the ground. Open up your crown center. Allow yourself to float upward. Your consciousness feels lighter, almost detached. Continue to float upward, never looking down, for about sixty seconds. Note how easy it is to move afterward.

AIR AMPLIFIER Stop talking and listening to anyone. Sit alone, if you can, taking deep, relaxed breaths. Sigh as you exhale. Your sound releases the blockages and obstacles around your air element. As you inhale, your lungs expand with clarity. Feel lighter and breezier as you continue. Continue for sixty seconds.

AIR DIMMER If you are feeling spacey, detached, or ungrounded, amplify your earth element. While doing so, put your hand on top of your head to cover your crown center. Hold for sixty seconds.

WATER AMPLIFIER You may want to find a private place to do this. Stand straight. Tilt your head upward by raising your chin just a few inches.

Take deep breaths, and on the exhale, either scream or moan. The scream will bring up your rage. The moan will bring up your sorrow, both of which block your emotional flow. Both will open up fear. Continue to release and try not to be afraid of anyone else's reactions. That is why you're blocked in the first place. Repeat for sixty seconds. You'll feel lighter and more peaceful afterward.

WATER DIMMER To correct a water element that is too active; that is, when you are overwhelmed with emotion, either ground yourself with the earth amplifier or open up to more rational energy with the air amplifier. Focusing on another element will allow you to swim out of deeper waters into more manageable flow.

To become more familiar with the elements and the qualities associated with them, check out the following chart. Your astrological sign will also indicate which element you are most at home with, and consequently, which element is likely to overwhelm you at times. (Chapter 5 will provide you with even more in-depth information on this.)

ELEMENTAL QUALITIES

FIRE	EARTH	AIR	WATER
Courage	Steadiness	Clarity	Depth
Anger	Security	Memory	Emotions
Passion	Nurturing	Thought	Rage
Will	Stillness	Concentration	Sorrow
Force	Fertility	Ideas	Fear
Survival	Trust	Understanding	Joy
Warmth	Comfort	Expression	Attachment
Light	Sensuality	Rationality	Fluidity

PSYCHIC POWER TRAVEL

Business travel is one of the most exhausting, demanding, and psychically challenging aspects of modern working life. I traveled a lot when I worked in advertising, and often travel to see clients now, so I have gotten the hang of setting up my own psychic space wherever I went.

You can apply your power tools to just about any part of the travel process, from clearing the way to the airport and finding a good parking space to making your plane. You don't have to stop there, either. If you're afraid of flying, you can use your powers to calm yourself.

The most exhausting part of travel, though, seems to be in trying to get a good night's sleep in a strange room. Although many hotel rooms are quite comfortable—they're quieter than home—the lighting and the energy are different, so it's basically a foreign environment.

PSYCHIC TRAVEL KITS

The easiest way to acclimate to a new place is to bring along some small power objects and a scent that reminds you of home. Little kids know exactly what they're doing when they insist on taking their teddy bears or blankets along to a foreign place. Why abandon this practice as an adult? You can anchor your energy in a room by merely placing a photograph of your family next to your bed, putting a crystal or stone on the dresser, spraying a fragrance around the room (or lighting incense), and unpacking your bags. This two-minute process will make you more psychically at home, and therefore more likely to relax.

I also pack a smudge stick so that I can cleanse the room of the energy of the previous occupants. To cleanse myself of plane energy, I usually have some sea salt with me for my shower. It may sound silly but it really helps keep me clear and focused on the road.

The most grueling trip I ever took was a book tour (and I think most authors will agree that these are real endurance tests). My first tour was in the dead of February, starting in Canada, plunging into the Midwest and then into Texas, followed by the West Coast. I think I saw ten cities in less than two weeks. I averaged two flights per day because of connections, often early in the morning and late at night, so that I could make morning radio shows, do print or TV interviews during the day, and then a bookstore appearance at night. In other words, sleep was a luxury and relaxation a fantasy, all while I was supposed to be charming, interesting, and lucid.

Fortunately, my travel power tools came in real handy. This was my standard kit:

White votive candle in its own holder

Incense sticks (stored inside my Filofax pocket)

Lavender in a pouch so I could have a whiff at hand

Meditation crystal

Hematite to stay grounded

Amethyst to stay spacious

Sea salt

Smudge stick

With my toolkit in hand, I would check into hotels, run to my room, light up my candle and incense, and breathe relief. It was like being in my living room for a second. Of course, meditating helped keep me steady, too.

I chuckle at the thought of the maid smelling my smudge stick and dumping the tiny ashes from my incense out of the water glass. I never know if I should ask for a smoking or non-smoking room, either. Who knows? Maybe the enlightened hotel of the new millennium will provide incense burners.

Remember to pack your power tools for your meetings or presentations, too. For use both at home and away, your psychic power tools are extremely portable and extremely effective.

Parking Spaces and Traffic Jams

I bet you want to know how to get that parking space, don't you? It's not hard but you have to start before you get into the car—in other words, if you're cruising the lot in desperation, it's too late to conjure that space.

As soon as you can, like the day you find out you're going away, start visualizing a smooth and easy trip. Use the following exercise for sending energy into the future. You need to give yourself time to set up a psychic scenario and to let it form. That's why it's just too late to pull up a parking space by the time you're in your car. Your own energy will be too tense and your personality too willful to send out any clear psychic message.

If you've forgotten or had no time to send energy into the future, use your tools to calm you down (breathe through your power centers) and stretch time if you need to. If you do meditate, it's useful to do so in a stressful situation.

Don't expect these exercises to make the Los Angeles rush hour disappear. By sending your energy into the future, you may end up taking a different route to work, passing the time more easily.

SENDING YOUR ENERGY
INTO THE FUTURE

Hold a power object and a clear crystal in your hand during this exercise.

Sit quietly, allowing your breathing to relax. Feel your third eye center and open it with deep purple light. Also open your heart energy with soft green light. Feel the light gliding in and out, back to front and front to back, of both energy centers.

Through your third eye, see the journey ahead of you. See the flow of traffic, the ease of parking, easy check-in, comfortable seat, quiet, easy trip. Feel the reality of each step of your trip. Breathe your heart energy into each scene.

Sit with this vision and this energy until you feel complete with it. Before you let it go, blow it into the future. Use your breath to gently send your vision and its feeling into the day and time and space on which you need it. Know that your power will meet you there. As you blow your vision into the future, touch or squeeze your power object, knowing that your vision is anchored within it.

When you are finished, open your eyes and put your hands firmly on the ground. You have just straddled your energy into the future, and you need to ground yourself back to the present. Allow yourself a few moments to gather yourself after the exercise.

In this exercise, you are psychically open to seeing the future—both in creating it and in watching it as it is approaching you. As you open up to your visualization, feel, sense, or see any resistance to any part of what you want. You may sense that traffic will be very bad, maybe that the plane will be delayed, or that your trip will be canceled altogether. As you do this exercise, you will find that you are very open to intuitive impressions. This doesn't mean that you should try to imagine what could happen when you travel; just carry on the exercise and see if you run into any impressions. Try to remember what you feel about your trip and see how accurate your impressions were.

I once traveled to Kennedy Airport in New York on my way to an international flight. I left in plenty of time, but got stuck in a nightmare of construction and traffic. Knowing it was too late to breathe any energy into the future, I instead tried to breathe power through the thick of traffic to open it up. I also decided to send some energy into the flight so that it might be delayed by half an hour, just to make sure I would make it.

I had a hard time divorcing my will (just wanting the cars to part like the Red Sea) from a more open state of psychic creativity, but the exercise did calm me down a bit. When I arrived at the airport, the monitor showed that the flight was delayed by thirty-five minutes, so both my baggage and I made the plane with a couple of minutes to spare.

CLEARING THROUGH TRAFFIC

This is best to do before your trip, but if you're in the car, and you're calm, you can try it. It can be most effective.

Close your eyes. Relax your breathing and your body as much as possible. Open your heart center with green light. Open your power center with yellow light. Breathe through them calmly.

Visualize sending their light ahead of you into the traffic, gently loosening up the density of cars and trucks. Keep your breathing relaxed. Know that the traffic breaks up and flows like the flow of your breath.

Send the elements ahead of you, one by one, clearing the path before you. Fire, cleansing a path for you, then earth, stabilizing and grounding your way, air to blow away obstructions, and water to cleanse and purify your path.

Allow each element to complete its task. Feel that element, be with it as it creates your psychic pathway.

> *When you feel complete, open your eyes. Keep your breathing as relaxed as possible. Close your heart center and your power center. Turn on your radio to ground yourself back into reality.*

I find that this exercise really does work, but not until your patience has hit the wall and you can't take one more second of traffic. After you give up and run through your repertoire of fruity curses, you're bound to succeed.

Even if you don't believe in this exercise, doing it will make you feel better and increase your psychic power attunement for that day. There's simply no downside to it.

Dealing with Waiting Lists and Standby

Most of us know when we're going to have to chance standby——when it's too late to make a change but we hope and pray we can hop on a later or earlier flight. The minute you know you want to secure a standby seat, grab a clear crystal (one that you use often) and breathe your energy into it through your heart center. After a minute or two of this, point your crystal upward to the sky, and ask aloud to send your energy onto the flight of your choice, with spaciousness and calm, for the greater good, and then put your crystal away. You can take it with you if you want—it's always a good tool to travel with.

This practice does one of two things: It will clear space for you if that is at all possible, and it will not clear space for you if that is not a good choice. Not that missing the flight foretells something bad for the airplane, but that it was either not necessary for you to go on the flight or it prevented you from dealing with an unforeseeable problem on the other end of your trip.

This also holds true also for waiting lists for hotels, tickets for events, and even restaurant reservations. If your psychic power is not enough to conjure what it is you want, you probably don't need it or you can do better.

I can't help but chuckle when I think of my own experience with this. I was trying to fly to Saint Louis to be early for a meeting, so I turned up at the airport for a flight leaving two hours before my ticket time. I decided to use my crystal to help me out, so I sent energy upward for getting on the flight, and went as far as to ask for a first class upgrade. I waited to hear the standby list, but my name was never called. I went to the desk and asked what had happened, and discovered that I had been kept on my original flight but was bumped up to first class. I shot a stern look at my crystal to see if it had cracked or something, but it had not.

I passed by the gate where I had waited to get on standby and noticed that the flight had not yet left. Passengers were coming *off* the plane, shaking their heads and lining up at the service counter. A mechanical problem had grounded the flight, and as a result, my flight was booked to capacity. There I was, secure with my first class seat, and thanking my crystal for its wondrous work!

Psychic Soothers for Nervous Fliers

There are so many power tools to assist you with safe flying that I can't possibly mention them all here. If I were a nervous flier, I'd start with a visualization of the journey ahead and bring my power objects with me, including a quartz crystal to loosen my energy for flying. There are many calming scents to carry, too, like lavender and vanilla.

Takeoff and landing provide excellent conditions for meditation. Use the hum of the engine, which can be quite lulling. Meditation is the most beneficial exercise you can do at any point during a flight. It will not only steady your nerves, but it can also help you arrive at your destination in a calm, collected state of mind.

A LAST WORD ON GENERAL PRACTICES

It's hard to always be open to the psychic skill you need to employ. You may stubbornly resist acknowledging that you constantly have trouble getting your energy going and would resist using the fire-amplifying techniques. You may decide that your recurring dream of car racing has no bearing on your life path, but simply shows an interest in attending next year's Indy 500. You may curse your travel agent with every travel plan you ever endured. You're only human.

However, a true executive mystic will always look for ways to enhance his or her experience and satisfaction. Identifying ways to improve yourself overall will inevitably spill over into your work life.

Be patient with yourself and be open to what your intuitive skills can do for you. You'll not only have fun practicing these techniques, nine times out of ten you'll have a positive experience as well.

◈ 5 ◈

PSYCHIC POWER
AND OTHER PEOPLE

So far, we've concentrated on getting your psychic power up to par, and if you've been using any of the techniques, you've already considerably improved your skills. You are more aware of your own power and how to work it; you can now begin using it to its fullest potential with other people.

One psychic power tool that can help you "psych others out" employs a basic understanding of zodiac signs, or the theory behind astrology. A second commonly used tool in business today that offers a look into someone else's psyche is graphology, or handwriting analysis. A fundamental understanding of both of these tools can help you:

- Anticipate strengths and weaknesses in others
- Communicate more clearly and strategically
- Foster better working relationships
- Assemble a power team

THE BUSINESS OF ASTROLOGY

Contrary to what you might think, astrology isn't a cheap way to pick up strangers. It's an ancient art of ascribing archetypal characteristics based on the configuration of planets and stars at the time of someone's birth. My consulting business, Executive Mystic, uses astrology consciously and successfully to help clients find their most satisfying career paths and to predict success. Rather than preach to you about the power of the stars, I will do here what I do for my clients: I will give you an astrological primer and let you be the judge.

The origin of astrology is generally attributed to the early Egyptians, but the twelve signs of the zodiac were identified and used by nearly all ancient civilizations. Noticing that every two hours a new constellation appeared in the sky, observers soon discovered that the stars formed an arc of twelve signs in a twenty-four-hour period. The sun, which appeared to rise "in" each of these constellations for about thirty days, also appeared to rise each day a little later in the constellation, traveling through each of the twelve signs in a year. The first zodiac sign was considered to be Aries (commencing on the vernal equinox on March 21), because it heralded spring and a new growing season.

Every astrological sign is associated not only with its constellation and archetype, but also with an element (fire, earth, air, or water), an energetic inclination (cardinal, fixed, or mutable), and a motivation or purpose.

Once you understand the characteristics of each sign, you will realize how useful astrology is in dealing with people, especially in the workplace. When I first learned how well it worked, it was almost impossible for me to meet people without asking them their birthday. In preparing for even the most formal business meetings, I would find out attendees' birthdays so that I could anticipate their needs, know how to talk to them, and avoid pressing their hot buttons.

Astrology by no means offers a way to control people's reactions, but it can alert you to how best to approach them, allay their fears, and develop a more productive working relationship. All this requires is a little skill and some basic understanding of the signs and what drives them.

Astrology as a Power Tool

If you have familiarized yourself with the basic elemental properties from the last chapter, you can easily apply them to each zodiac sign. If you find yourself interviewing an earth sign, for example, you know not to judge him or her harshly for non-assertive communication skills, but you will welcome his or her steady devotion. If you're looking to put together a team for an important new project, you'll want to make certain that all the elements are represented so that you achieve the right balance of creativity, energy, actions, and follow-through.

Refresh your knowledge with the elemental chart on page 118 so that you can easily interpret each sign's characteristics.

Cardinal, Fixed, Mutable

A less familiar but equally significant property associated with zodiac signs is their energetic motivation. A sign that is **cardinal** means that it likes to move in one direction, like an arrow. Aries, Cancer, Libra, and Capricorn are cardinal signs. These individuals are very intrigued and motivated by one purpose or task and they will not stop until it is complete (you might want to stay out of their way until it is). To get something done, consider using a cardinal sign.

The next energetic type is the **fixed** sign. Fixed signs—Taureans, Leos, Scorpios, and Aquarians—do not like change. It takes an enormous amount of energy of all forms—physical, emotional, passionate, intellectual, and psychic—for them to respond to change, even if it is in their best interest and they know it. Fixed signs are loyal, patient, and full of fortitude. They rule staffs, teams, or companies very well, and look after their people with compassion, but have a hard time implementing programs they do not fully support. Stubborn types, these signs do it their way or not at all.

No one gets off easy, even the **mutable** signs. Mutable signs shift easily, to the point where they can move in practically all directions all the time. Although flexibility is valuable, you won't find much steadiness here. Being a member of this type, I know the pitfalls of mutability (you can see everything from all sides, which makes it hard to make a decision) and the positives (you can always find a bright side). Watch for waffling on issues and excess energy from Geminis, Virgos, Sagittarians, and Pisces, but expect to see lots of ideas flowing and a little added spark to your group.

The Elements Rule

In astrology, the four elements—fire, earth, air, and water—represent or rule different professions. It can be useful to know how the elements come into play so that you can better assess your own strengths as well as those of your staff or colleagues. If you are most comfortable with water energy, for example, you should be aware of how you relate to fire-fueled professions. (You can use the elemental amplifiers or dimmers in the previous chapter to help you out if you need them.) Here is a sample of each element's general domain.

Fire represents creativity, passion, risk-taking, and aggressive activity; rules foreign ventures, electronics, entertainment, healing professions, theater, supervisory roles, machining, mechanical operations.

Earth represents physical things and money; rules banking, commodity investing, jewelry, real estate, mining, gardening, biotechnology, fashion, clergy, farming, masonry.

Air represents intellectual pursuits and exchanges, writing; rules communications, law, teaching, distribution, transportation, printing.

Water represents intuition and imagination; rules shipping, navigating, aquatics, fishing, beverages, hotel and restaurant management, medicine, security, music.

Zodiac Archetypes

Each sign also has a motivation or purpose that is characteristic of a lifetime goal or mission statement. Look for your sign on the chart and check yours out. I would be surprised if it seemed odd or ill fitting.

SIGN	ELEMENT	ENERGY	INNATE PURPOSE
Aries (3/21–4/19)	Fire	Cardinal	I like a challenge and I will get things done.
Taurus (4/20–5/20)	Earth	Fixed	I have an eye for design and quality, and I acquire valuables.
Gemini (5/21–6/21)	Air	Mutable	I enjoy learning, and share information and ideas well.
Cancer (6/22–7/22)	Water	Cardinal	I have uncanny senses and I take business personally.
Leo (7/23–8/22)	Fire	Fixed	I enjoy the spotlight and am a natural born leader.
Virgo (8/23–9/22)	Earth	Mutable	I am a great problem solver and I'm very resourceful.
Libra (9/23–10/23)	Air	Cardinal	I resolve conflict and I am very judicious.

Scorpio (10/24–11/21)	Water	Fixed	I play things close to the chest and I'm very creative and passionate.
Sagittarius (11/22–12/21)	Fire	Mutable	I take risks and explore new ideas and theories.
Capricorn (12/22–1/19)	Earth	Cardinal	I am tenacious, dedicated, and devoted to achieving.
Aquarius (1/20–2/18)	Air	Fixed	I am a forward thinker, and a great teacher.
Pisces (2/19–3/20)	Water	Mutable	I am creative, imaginative, and hopeful for the future.

Although it is always important not to categorize people simply based on their astrological sign, it's helpful to familiarize yourself with each sign's predominant trait. Your chart, like those of others, is really a complex combination of astrological influences beyond the sun sign, which causes some people to claim, "I'm not really very Pisces-like," or "I'm not a classic Libra." That is to some degree true, but most often you will still find some strong traits that correspond to their sun sign.

Arians are generally willful, purposeful individuals who have a hard time reporting to anybody. They eventually find a way to circumvent authority, go into professions that allow them a lot of freedom, or start their own businesses. Being stuck in subordinate positions for too long can breed one passive-aggressive Aries.

Taurus individuals like steadiness, practical solutions, and good value for their money. They may not welcome change, but when it is proved to be worthy, they will work hard to embrace it. The Taurus weakness is usually in communications skills; as a general rule they need to learn to speak their piece as well as do a good job.

Geminis can look as if they are never paying attention but are often taking it all in at once. They are the first to admit to becoming easily distracted, and can get pretty cranky if there isn't enough to do or if the work is repetitive. Geminis need to learn to pause, smell the roses, and stop making trouble for the sake of some action.

Cancers love nurturing and security, and tend to seek out positions that offer them both. They are not the adventurers of the zodiac, and shrink from interpersonal risk, but can be greatly reliable in a crisis. They are highly consistent individuals and are quick to support others.

Leos are born to lead and can be counted on to add life to any meeting. Just take caution when you try to assign them what they may consider "menial" tasks. The king only likes to mix with the peasants on his terms, even if he is only a secretary. Make even small jobs important and the Leo will thrive.

Virgos, even the messiest Virgos, know how to cut to the chase, and exhibit some practical, efficient, and enlightened qualities in any task, from changing the toner on the printer to reorganizing the computer system for the year 2000. Be watchful of their critical eyes, though, and do not let their good deeds go unnoticed.

Libras are always good for lending a clear point of view on any subject, and have excellent intellectual resources to draw from. Just don't put too much pressure on them to make decisions, because they will stall until the issue goes away or blows up. They are diplomats, not warriors.

Scorpios are intense, private, and creative. Lighthearted goofing, though, is not easy going for them. Always respect Scorpios and their work, and they will be staunch supporters. Put Scorpios on the spot, however, and you'll lose them forever.

Sagittarians cannot abide sameness, so beware if you have repetitive work for this knowledge-hungry sign. They will pursue their goals like well-aimed arrows, but they will fall off the track once the thrill of the chase is gone. They make for great entrepreneurs in start-ups, but are weak on staying power.

Capricorns are the astrological masters of the universe, holding all the qualities we love to see in business: a shrewd practical nature, conservative but consistent ambition, and a desire for constant achievement. However, their devotion to their profession could weaken their humor, interpersonal skills, and ability to relax and have fun.

Aquarians are best at forecasting, inventing, and teaching, and their fixed nature can make them good, steady mentors. As they are so comfortable in the future, however, they tend to be weak in practical applications and work that requires constancy. They need to roam in their minds, if not in their jobs.

Pisces is such a creative, mutable sign that Pisceans often become impeccably organized to overcompensate. They are wonderful "people people" and could sell a bridge to its owner. Even in business, they need to be appreciated and psychically supported in order to thrive.

Astrological Team Building

Now that you're aware of the sharp contrast in personality and motivation among the twelve signs, you can see why, when consulting for businesses, I often do astrological audits. When a company or team isn't working well together, it is not all that surprising to find many of the same element or an obvious dearth of another.

One small advertising agency I analyzed was filled with Geminis (naturals in communications) and Leos (at home in entertainment and born leaders). This was excellent for the group's creativity, but the lack of earth signs (practicality and groundedness) hinted at a lack of order and financial prowess. That agency has since folded.

Another team I evaluated was at a software company. They had a nice balance of water and earth, with primarily Pisces, Cancers, and Virgos. They had one or two fire-driven employees but not a single air sign. In a conference with the senior management, I explained that the lack of the air element accounted for ineffective and unclear communications on both an intellectual and "common sense" level. They acknowledged that their company literature—in the form of brochures, a press kit, and fact sheets—had become a big problem, and was being bounced from one partner to another to be finished. I encouraged them to hire a professional writer and designer so that they could experience the talent of air. I hooked them up with one of the many freelancers I know (this one a Libra), who successfully helped them verbalize their services.

Once you've assembled your power team, consider the characteristics of your collective elemental makeup. If you're hiring someone new, you can find out their birthday (without the year) by asking when it is for the company list. Some of my more aggressive clients simply ask, "What sign are you?" in the interview. If you're too shy to do that, set up the question with your assistant or the receptionist. I know one executive who made his receptionist ask all visitors their sign on the pretext of being a beginning astrologer. (I was amused to learn that the receptionist did take an interest and is now an excellent astrologer.)

In building a creative, action-oriented, highly productive team, remember these general rules:

Water signs are very creative but not very practical.

Most fixed signs won't warm to new routines or big changes.

Too many air signs? Nervous energy, a lot of ideas, and no way of making them real.

Lots of mutable people make coming to consensus impossible.

Fire signs tend toward independence and don't always play well with others.

Earth signs are terrifically grounded—a great foil for water and air—but too many and you've got stability but not a lot of movement.

Cardinal signs are certain to get things done but aren't always keen on cooperation.

These are only a few examples of the kinds of imbalances you can have in a team. If you're stuck with an elemental imbalance, you can at least be alert to each sign's weaknesses and work to compensate for them. Also, it helps to stock your offices with the missing element.

- Give everyone mini Zen rock gardens to add earth if you're lacking. Be sure to get simple financial updates semimonthly to stay reality-based.
- To amplify the water element, buy a large aquarium or a few goldfish to feed water, and keep an ongoing dialogue with employees regarding their personal lives and emotional states.
- Put in full-spectrum lightbulbs or splashes of yellow to the decor to add to fire.
- Keep air circulating—provide a weekly newsletter or E-mail, or hold a weekly staff meeting to keep everyone apprised of what's going on.

You can easily shift a team in favor of one element or quality, but be sure that a couple of others are still represented. For instance, financial businesses may benefit primarily from many earth signs, but need fire signs to take risks, air signs to disseminate information, and water signs to sense where the market is going. Each zodiac sign brings a useful quality to a team.

Astrological One-on-Ones

Astrology is a great tool when you're meeting someone new. I have often called secretaries in advance of meeting their bosses to find out the executive's birthday (on the pretense of putting them on a birthday list). I found this extremely useful in knowing how to best communicate with them. Use the chart on elemental characteristics on page 118 and your knowledge of each sign's qualities to help guide you to a successful meeting.

Here's a little cheat sheet:

MEETINGS BY THE STARS

EXECUTIVE SIGN	DO'S	DON'TS
Aries	Allow them to lead if they want to. Allow them to solve a problem.	Don't interrupt or override with your own anecdotes.
Taurus	Prop your meeting environment well— make it comfortable and nice.	Don't talk too much or get too pushy. Don't expect an answer right away.
Gemini	Talk and listen. Keep the energy up and the boredom down.	Don't get too bogged down in details unless asked for them.
Cancer	Move low and slow— ease into camaraderie when it is offered.	Don't overwhelm with words or ideas. Listen and ask first.

EXECUTIVE SIGN	DO'S	DON'TS
Leo	Warmth and respect will make them at ease. Consider meeting in a room with natural light.	Don't dominate the meeting even if you are the expert. Decisions should be made by them.
Virgo	Have detailed info in your head or at hand if needed. Be informed and alert.	Don't expose too many problems or anxieties. Don't have a messy or dirty environment.
Libra	Show the ability to understand partnership. Allow for their point of view and lively discussion.	Don't get aggressive or ask for a commitment. Don't expose a harsh point of view.
Scorpio	Create a safe and relaxed meeting space. Know your stuff well.	Don't even think of being intimate too soon. Don't be too casual.
Sagittarius	Keep the meeting as short as possible and cover essentials. Include anything new and different.	Don't allow it to run overtime and keep to few details unless requested otherwise.

EXECUTIVE SIGN	DO'S	DON'TS
Capricorn	Show respect and appreciation for hard work. Recognize achievement if possible.	Don't blow your own horn. Don't go on about other people.
Aquarius	Allow for opinions of all sorts. Consider deeper issues, ask questions.	Don't pass judgment, just offer a point of view. Don't be too "by the book."
Pisces	Make your meeting environment safe and nonthreatening. Allow for a loose agenda.	Don't intrude on personal space and don't expect to get a lot done right away.

Observe how you see the zodiac playing out around you but don't get mired in it. It is simply another highly effective psychic power tool, like the others in this book, to help you tune in to other people's energy.

If you want the full scope of your chart (or someone else's), you need a practiced astrologer. To find an astrologer, look into your local New Age bookstore or do a little research at the library. There are numerous astrologers in every community, and if you don't mind asking around, you're likely to get some good recommendations from colleagues or friends. Talk to the astrologer on the phone for a bit before you make an appointment, however, and use your intuition to see if you feel comfortable with the way he or she sounds. There are many excellent professionals in this area, but personalities and styles vary. Go with your gut on this one.

AND SO IT IS WRITTEN: GRAPHOLOGY

Separate from the stars and perhaps even more widely accepted in the corporate world is *graphology*, or handwriting analysis. Graphology, the scientific study of handwriting, is used broadly by human resources departments, police, banks, and enterprising managers in a variety of industries, not just for identifying individuals but also for predicting behavior.

WHAT WRITING SAYS ABOUT YOU

Graphology uses an individual's script (usually in the form of a short letter on unlined paper) to see personality characteristics, strengths and weaknesses. You've probably heard people say that you can't judge a book by its cover, which is exactly why graphology is so revealing. Most of us can appear to be a strong, competent corporate player—especially for an interview—but do we really have the wherewithal to be one?

Graphology offers profound insights into the personality beyond the barriers of physical or verbal defenses.

Because people rarely work at having a particular kind of handwriting (with the exception of forgers, who are often foiled by graphologists anyway), you can get a true view of a personality, beyond the trappings of a power suit. If you're the one being analyzed, make sure to use your psychic power tools so that your handwriting passes the test.

How Does It Work?

Graphology compares an individual's handwriting to the original penmanship taught in school, the Palmer Cursive technique. The deviation between what you were taught and how your writing looks now is where your personality traits are seen.

You can use some simple graphology techniques to get a glimpse into people's characters, to gauge whether they have the kind of personality that would work well in a team, to determine whether they are positive thinkers and whether they're aggressive, passive, or reflective.

Many companies use graphology as a sole screening device for personnel issues and regularly use the services of a professional graphologist. There are many highly trained individuals whose expertise can save you a lot of time and money, and who can identify many subtleties not mentioned here.

Simple Graphology

There are some aspects to handwriting that you can examine in order to better interpret others' personalities. Be sure to look at the big picture after you identify each aspect, though, as you'll probably start to see a predominant theme. Resist the desire to make assumptions about people based solely on one or two qualities of their handwriting. An overall perspective is the only way to get realistic insight into a personality.

Remember, it is best to obtain a sample of the individual's handwriting on unlined paper, in the form of a note, complete with a signature. As a test, why not look at your own writing? Address a note to someone with a proper salutation: "Dear _____." Then write a two- or three-line message, and sign it "Sincerely, _____." Check out your writing against the criteria described below and see if it reveals the real you.

USE OF SPACE My favorite graphologist asserts that use of space is one of the most important traits to examine, and one that crosses all language and cultural boundaries—it's even relevant in Chinese and Japanese writing. How you use the space on a blank piece of paper shows a lot about how you feel around other people and how you behave socially.

The use of space on the page is an indication of how comfortable you (or the person you're analyzing) are with attention.

Words crammed into the corner of a page, particularly if the writing and signature are small, are an indication of someone who doesn't want to be the focus of attention. Large letters that take up lots of space indicate a love of the limelight, as does using the whole page and spreading the words around. Subordinate positions with little direct responsibility may bore those whose big writing indicates a craving for attention.

The closer one's words are to the others, the more closeness a person needs. If words overlap or lines run into each other, the person has problems setting or keeping boundaries. Overlapping letters often indicate symbiotic tendencies—these people won't give you space and they don't know when to stop. Avoid hiring assistants or partners who exhibit these tendencies unless you, too, favor blurry boundaries.

Large spaces between words and lines indicate a need for space. Keep this in mind for self-starters and positions that require self-reliance and little supervision.

Those who are truly self-aware rarely have spacing problems—they leave room on the page to write exactly what they want and don't end up overlapping anything. This measured, even style indicates a thoughtful, well-balanced, organized employee.

SIZE OF WORDS As you might've guessed, large-size words signal people who like—and perhaps need—lots of attention. Does the handwriting take up the whole page and is the signature large, too? If so, this person may have a "larger than life" personality; keep an eye out for other clues that may indicate a melodramatic or emotionally immature individual. In contrast, smaller words indicate a more low-key, low-profile type. You can apply these same analogies to see if the personality fits the job.

SIZE OF CAPITAL LETTERS Large caps call attention to a person (look at me!). They indicate good self-esteem, and not necessarily a big ego. If you like working with people who don't demand too much support and feedback, look for this trait. However, they may think better of themselves than you do, so observe how they handle your criticism—check their loops, as described next.

LOOPS In American cursive writing we were taught to make elliptical loops for many letters. When these loops are big, it indicates that the person tends to be emotional. When loops are elongated or nonexistent, that indicates a lack of fulfillment. A strong slash downward can mean determination or anger.

Any extension, whether it is a loop or a letter that reaches up like a *t*, can be of interest in analyzing your subject, particularly if it is pronounced. Whether a letter reaches sharply up or down, it shows the individual's tendencies toward extremes; that is, if they believe in something, they go all the way. This can be a good trait for a cause-related job.

It's common to find a few different loops in a person's writing. Go with what predominates—that characteristic is more important.

If you see a lot of unfinished loops or slashing letters, you probably have an angry person on your hands—proceed with caution. In determining whether this anger is something that will affect their work, you can use your intuition or you can simply ask about their prior employment. If you sense that there's unresolved hostility there, you may want to consider how this may or may not work for your company.

SLANT In elementary school, we are taught to slant our writing to the right. Those people who carry on this rightward slant through adulthood tend to be forward thinking, progressive extroverts, good managers.

Upright handwriting shows a need for objectivity, and can indicate immutability.

When writing slants backwards, it shows a resistance to change or reflects a person who is more withdrawn. These personalities are traditionalists who prefer the status quo, or are in opposition to new ideas. They can make good industry watch-dogs, as they tend to be skeptics and can offer balancing energy to an office that has too many mavericks.

DOTS OF *I*'S AND CROSSES OF *T*'S Just like the slant, if the dot of the *i* or the cross of the *t* occurs to the right of the letter, the individual is ambitious and innovative. This is true only for the English language.

SIGNATURES Interestingly, an illegible signature often indicates vagueness, someone who doesn't want to be pinned down, doesn't want to give anything away, or someone who desires privacy. Hard-to-read signatures are common to lawyers, diplomats, and doctors for this very reason.

It is rare for the signature to match the rest of the handwriting. These people really are who they say they are—what you see is what you get. Most often, though, a signature has been consciously or unconsciously crafted—it is no more telling than a mask or a facade. Your signature tells people what you want them to think you are.

Look at your signature. Is it bigger than the name of the addressee of the letter? If so, you need more space than you are willing to give other people (i.e., you think you're more important).

If you signed your note to the right of the text, you're people-oriented and inclined to reach out to others. You're probably also a risk-taker and not averse to change.

If your signature is positioned to the left, you prefer tradition to progress. In the middle of the page, it can indicate belief in balance and moderation.

THE USE OF ZONES In the space where we write, there are three zones: the upper zone, where letters extend upward, as in a *b*; the middle zone, where letters rest on the baseline, like an *a*; and the lower zone, for letters that extend downward, like *g* and *p*.

Look at the zones in your handwriting to see if there is a relative balance of spacing. If one zone is dramatically different from the others, it's another indication of extremes in one's personality. If your use of zones is unusual—for instance, if you flat-line all of your letters, or you fill a large upper zone or a large lower zone—that is an indication of some imbalance in your personality. It is best not to assign a meaning to the zone in question. A strong lower zone doesn't indicate you have a "downer" personality. Zones simply indicate that there is likely to be some extreme in the personality, which could warrant further probing to find out what it is.

CONNECTING YOUR LETTERS Connecting letters indicates excellent follow-through, follow-up, and systematic thinking. That's good for synthesizing ideas. (Watch for fuzzy boundaries if the connecting letters overlap. These people don't know when to go home.) Breaks between letters reflect independence and intuition.

Here is one style model:

A **thinking** type of personality has an upright slant (objective) and connected letters (thoroughness). This is a plus for scientists, researchers, doctors, historians, and other professions that analyze and synthesize a great deal of information.

Intuitive types have original letter formation plus unconnected letters and a mild slant to the right. They often make up their own style of writing, a combination of printing and cursive. You are bound to find this writing in creative professions of all kinds and entrepreneurs.

A **sensing** type is a "doer" with a strong middle zone, a right slant, and strong extensions to the right. These types connect their letters. This writing would indicate good salesmanship and service (in terms of customers and support staff).

Feeling people draw big loops when they write. If the loops are really big, you have a very emotional person on your hands (check out a teenage girl's handwriting if there's any doubt).

There may also be letters that are unconnected. Depending on how large the loops are (too large is probably too much for any profession), vocations that provide nurturing or emotional support are good for this type of personality—nursing, social work, child care. In addition, this kind of writing tends to change over time as we become emotionally more mature.

ILLEGIBLE HANDWRITING When handwriting is illegible, such as when a word is only partially written out and then finished by a squiggly or straight line—it is indicative of someone who doesn't want to be pinned down. Perhaps he or she is very private or perhaps this means you are dealing only with the superficial side of the personality. When the writing becomes even less legible, there may be negative implications, like unscrupulousness or forgery.

If You Don't Like What You See

Obviously, if you see something in a person's handwriting that causes you concern, you may think it is necessary to investigate further—or simply not offer that person the job. However, if you have no concerns about performance, at the very least you have some insight into the person's secret self. If you are worried about performance, and the handwriting confirms your suspicions, take some time to discuss it with a trained human resources professional. Above all, don't feel forced to act on your conclusions at all—if you're not sure, keep an eye out to see if these patterns portend issues to come.

If you see something in your own handwriting that causes you concern, you can actually change your writing and, as a result, change your personality.

By analyzing your handwriting, you may become aware that you are afraid of change, seemingly superficial, or poor at follow-through.

If you consciously alter the appropriate elements of your handwriting, you can actually change your behavior.

Here's how to do it:

1. Be aware of the attitude or trait your handwriting shows.
2. Accept it. Resisting the truth is just a form of denial that will keep you from getting what you want.
3. *Consistently* change the handwriting for twenty-one days Like physical exercise, it doesn't work if you only do it once in a while.

When you consciously and continually make the effort to change your writing, you will also see a change in your behavior. One graphology professional proposes that by altering your handwriting, you are visually reorienting and reprogramming your brain.

Hiring by Handwriting

One professional graphologist in the market for a personal assistant ran a personal ad in her local paper. In addition to a résumé, she requested a handwritten cover letter. Her fax machine was inundated with applications, and of the eighty-five résumés she received, she interviewed only three people. The handwriting samples were the first screener, and she looked at the résumés afterward. So far her hire has worked out nicely.

There are many more details and subtleties in deciphering handwriting than are presented here, and you'll want to be sure that you know what you're getting. Even if you have a great book on handwriting analysis, I do not suggest that you rely solely on your individual interpretation for a hiring decision. You'll need a combination of experience and training to gain confidence in your decisions. You can always use a professional to guide you in your assumptions.

However, you can use handwriting as just one of several hiring tools, to broaden your screening process. In this case, your individual judgment would probably be a safe bet.

CHOOSING A PSYCHIC POWER TEAM

How would you handle this situation? You are the team management leader of a task force for attracting new business for your company, a sports shoe manufacturer. You have four team members, one from each of four disciplines (sales, production, distribution, and design) already assigned to you, and you can ask one or two more people to join the team. Your company has given you a small budget and the added incentive of a team bonus pool based on the number of new accounts you can attract. Your team breaks down as follows:

Member	Sign	Handwriting Summary
You	Taurus	Upright, medium-size, small loops, good use of space
Sales	Aries	Slanted right, strong upper zone, uneven use of space
Production	Leo	Upright, good loops, mix of cursive and printing
Distribution	Libra	Small, right slanting, small caps and loops
Design	Pisces	Slight slant to the right, good loops, dots and crosses to the right of letters

You've now met with your core team members once. What would you be inclined to add to this mix?

Although there is no "right" answer, you may want to consider a few supplementing energies. The first place I'd start is with you. You are a Taurus with upright handwriting. Do you feel that you are inclined to take risks and/or pioneer new territory? If you know in your heart this is not your forte, go for a new team member, maybe a junior management executive who can bring some "adventurer" energy to the team. Look for a Gemini, Sagittarius, Aquarian, or Aries, and check for right-slanting handwriting and clues to forward thinking. If you want to add another salesperson, you can apply these same qualities, but beware of boundary issues that are sure to appear with the already appointed Aries whose handwriting indicates some territorial sensitivities.

If you do amplify these energies on your team, you may want to balance it by adding a financial person to make sure the schemes you come up with are indeed viable. Try not to lean too heavily in either direction or you'll lose the synergy of a diverse team.

With a rudimentary knowledge of astrology and graphology, you can put together a team that will work together cohesively and creatively. You can also shift the balance to achieve what you want, whether it be stability, innovation, growth, or knowledge.

Psychic Power Complements and Supplements

As you have your own powers, skills, and gifts, so do others. In business especially you will surely benefit from others who can complement you with their different gifts and supplement your strengths when you are forming a team.

In my consulting experience, I have seen many different combinations of psychic energies. There is really no bad combination but there are some that are more efficient, more productive, and more powerful.

The head of corporate communications for a medium-size company I consult for (and a Capricorn) told me recently he was pleased with his handpicked PR people, but that he was put off by some inconsistencies in their internal communications, and that he was having trouble scheduling weekly status meetings with them. I asked him to look up their signs, which was easy to do with his company's birthday list at his fingertips. I laughed out loud when I saw that they were *all* Geminis. This is a typical sign for public relations, because it is all about information and communication. Although I complimented my client for picking the right astrological types, I explained that this was precisely why he was having trouble.

Gemini is a restless air sign that likes to move around (therefore, getting all three people together is inherently difficult). Gemini is also mutable, which can indicate changes right up until the last minute—this can cause inconsistencies. Rather than disrupt his team on an astrological note, I asked my friend to relinquish his structured Capricorn preferences and play on the Gemini turf: request E-mail updates instead of meeting in person, call a monthly meeting on Monday mornings to go over glitches, and meet one-on-one when necessary. I also recommended he pay attention to astrological balance if possible. A Cancer, Virgo, or Scorpio would be equally good at PR and add a different element and energy to his mercurial team.

Although this executive was reluctant to embrace astrology as a real team-building tool, he tried my recommendation and found it worked. He now regularly refers people to my firm, the highest compliment a Capricorn can pay.

If you're working with a group of people and you don't have the ability to pick and choose, you can use your knowledge of writing and the stars to better balance your group.

Figure out your team's zodiac signs and associated attributes. This will give you insight into what motivates them and what makes them crazy. If you have a Scorpio boss, respect privacy, but if the boss is a Sagittarian, go for familiarity. If you have problems working with other people, just knowing the basic qualities of their sign can make communicating with them easier.

Elisa complained that she just didn't get the recognition she felt she deserved. As an Aries salesperson at a wholesale jewelry manufacturer, she had excellent energy and commitment to bring in new accounts. She was considering whether to register her dissatisfaction to her boss (Sheila, a Cancer), or to just look for another job. Elisa's frustration was growing but she didn't know how to deal with it.

Elisa's reluctance to deal with Sheila face-to-face was not typical for an Aries. Let's review the dynamics of this situation using astrology and handwriting:

Elisa	Sheila
Aries (I like a challenge)	Cancer (I care)
Cardinal	Cardinal
Fire	Water
Small writing	Medium-size writing
Slanted to the right	Upright
Pointy, extended loops	Big loops
Used all the space	Used upper half of paper
Signed right of center	Signed in the center

This may look like an indecipherable hodgepodge of information, but it holds some interesting insights.

Both Elisa and Sheila have cardinal energy, which is the commitment to proceed in one direction. Presuming they apply this to work, they are both dedicated to getting the job done. This is an important commonality.

Elisa's Aries archetype is confrontational and aggressive, task-oriented. Sheila's Cancer archetype is more sensitive and nurturing.

Elisa is very much a fire element, seemingly ready to go out and fight for her cause. This would account for the anger, but not for her inability to deal with it. Sheila's watery Cancer nature may make her more understanding and able to help Elisa deal with her intensity, but Elisa would have to ask for help.

Sheila's handwriting shows an emotional but objective personality. This indicates that she could be open to understanding and considering Elisa's point of view. Her use of space also signifies that she does not seek the spotlight and approaches it cautiously.

Elisa, though interested in moving toward the future, reveals some intensity in her extended pointy loops. Her small writing shows that she is not comfortable drawing attention to herself, although she is comfortable with her place in the organization.

After Elisa looked at this analysis, she reconsidered her approach. She knew it was best to see Sheila in person, and that her fear of expressing her dissatisfaction had to be faced. Elisa dabbed on a little carnation scent for protection and wore a wool rose-colored jacket to help her psychic subtext communicate gentleness. She also put her power amulet, a solid gold sunflower charm, into her pocket.

She decided to state her case in a calm, relaxed manner, so that she would not lose her temper. She tried out this empathetic statement:

"I feel as if I am not recognized for my achievements and it makes me feel demotivated." The use of the word *feel* here was a conscious decision.

Elisa was justly rewarded. Sheila told her that there was a bonus in the works but because it had not yet been fully approved, she hadn't wanted to say anything about it (caution is also a Cancerian trait). Furthermore, she said she was sorry that Elisa felt demotivated and wrote a special memo to the board about her superior performance.

Elisa was pleased by the results of this meeting and still uses her new knowledge in the way she communicates with Sheila; she also watches her own handwriting to see if her anger has shifted.

Astrological power tools and graphology are excellent power tools for knowing how to deal with conflict, and what is sometimes more important, knowing when to back off.

◄ 6 ◄

PSYCHIC POWER
TO IMPRESS

Psychic power tools can be combined in many ways to bring about smooth business interactions and help you get what you want. I find them most useful in meeting people for the first time, in public speaking, and in dealing with a difficult audience, be it in a sales pitch, a marketing meeting, or a new product launch. You should use them anytime you're dealing with people during your workday. They're guaranteed to help you influence even an unwilling audience and are useful for cutting short a lengthy or uncomfortable situation. This chapter will specifically address how to combine your knowledge and skills to make a powerful impression.

THE PSYCHIC POWER OF WORDS (OR, THE NEW PC: PSYCHICALLY CORRECT LANGUAGE)

With your psychic power tools in place, you are now ready to concentrate on the actual words you are saying, for even the most basic business vernacular can be laced with strong subtext. Although words cannot be called tools per se, they are inarguably a signficant source of psychic power. Take, for example, some common business terms that we often say without thinking:

"I'm on a deadline."

"This is the drop-dead date."

These phrases instill a strong psychic subtext of fear either in you, as the speaker, or in the listener. Either way, it's not psychically productive to operate from a fearful place, even if it's unconscious. I immediately trained myself not to use the term *deadline* when I started to write books. The psychic power of coming up to a deadline is totally unnerving—who wants to get to the *end of the line*, much less add the word *dead* to the concept, just because you're finishing a project? I traded *deadline* in for *due date*. Now it's more like giving birth than dropping dead.

More phrases with negative psychic power smacks:

"It's signed in blood."

"Heads will roll."

"My ass is on the line."

"I got my head handed to me."

Stay away from the grizzly or morbid when describing a situation, particularly to a boss, a client, or someone you're trying to impress. You could incite drama where none is needed, and you could be perceived as an alarmist. Powerful people often use understatement to convey their strength.

Your speech can also cause unnecessary psychic distress in others. One of my wiser, more experienced friends was horrified to hear someone say, "We're going to terminate him." She aptly pointed out that the *person* wasn't going to be terminated, his *job* was. When you associate termination with the end of life itself, your perspective is definitely askew, as is your work/life balance when your *job* equals *you*.

Although some words have stubbornly implanted themselves in our business culture, you can make a conscious effort not to use them. Some people, like headhunters, would be pleased (try *recruiter* instead). When you've reprogrammed your vocabulary away from routine expressions or industry slang, you'll free up some dormant creative flow in finding new names, and you may even coin a few new nontoxic phrases—a real sign of influence.

PSYCHIC ONE-ON-ONES

Diana, a client, was going to interview for a new job. She had excellent qualifications for selling real estate and wanted to work for one of New York's competitive top firms, but all of her past experience was in a community outside of Baltimore. She was concerned that she wouldn't come off as savvy and sophisticated as she assumed most New Yorkers were. After our consultation, she assembled a psychic power toolkit and set off for her meetings.

Diana prepared herself with a fragrance of success (she chose poppy) and made a charm for confidence using a yellow cotton cloth, some citrine crystals, and ginger. For her power outfit, she splurged on a good designer wool suit in a red jewel tone in order to communicate passion for her work. Before leaving for her first interview, she centered herself with a brief breathing meditation, then opened three power centers: throat for clear self-expression, heart to add softness to her cause and to forge a connection with her interviewer, and power to emit confidence and success.

POWER FRAGRANCES

SCENT	WHAT IT SAYS
Almond	I am prosperous.
Carnation	I have powerful energy.
Lavender	I am not judgmental.
Mint	I am good at attracting business.
Patchouli	I have peace of mind.
Pine	I am grounded.
Poppy	I am successful.
Rosemary	I am self-assured.
Rose	I am nice and gentle.
Sandalwood	I am intuitive.
Vanilla	I am warm and open.

The first man she interviewed with was a fast-talking, impatient person who looked at his watch as she entered his office and announced that he had very little time. This threw Diana off, as she'd never been greeted so abruptly or rudely in a business situation. Before she could get her energy settled in her seat, he immediately questioned her background to establish possible connections to New Yorkers (of which she had none), and then probed her to see how "upscale" her Baltimore experience had been. Although Diana had prepared herself for this very confrontation, she squirmed and stuttered, having lost her center. She recalled the dialogue to me:

> INTERVIEWER: So, what can you tell me about your connections here in the New York real estate market?
> DIANA: Well, I, uh, as you know, I don't have direct connections per se, but I'm very quick to get to know new places and, uh . . .
> INTERVIEWER: What relevant experience do you bring with you?
> DIANA: I've cracked tough markets before and I can . . .
> INTERVIEWER: What makes you think this is a tough market? New York is money for the asking. All you need to know is which buttons to push and you're rich.

By this point in the conversation, Diana just wanted to leave. She felt her interviewer was hostile and patronizing and sensed in her gut that this was not the kind of personality she would work well with. Gathering her dignity with a deep breath drawn from her solar plexus center, she squeezed her confidence charm in her pocketbook and stood up, taking leave before being asked to. Diane knew she had not effectively used her power tools in this interview and needed to rethink her strategy.

For her second appointment, Diana prepared the same way, but this time she opened her third eye center, too, to give her insight during the interview and to help her respond more intuitively to another brash personality. She was not surprised to meet another tough New Yorker, and although his questions were similar to her first interviewer's, she had done some quick but crucial psychic homework upon entering his office. She centered herself first and immediately made a quick appraisal of his workspace. She noted a framed dollar bill and some gold paperweights and listened closely as his first question confirmed her impression that he was a bottom-line kind of guy. When the interviewer asked if she knew how many brokers his firm had and how many homes it turned over, she cut to the chase, responding with impressive financial knowledge about the firm, including percentage of closings above market value, profit growth, and other information showing that she had done her homework. "Mr. Bottomline," as she dubbed him, was duly impressed. Sensing that she had successfully engaged him with that answer, she fingered the confidence charm in her suit pocket, took a deep breath, and turned the tables to her advantage. She leaned forward, sending her third eye energy to him, and asked *him* questions, such as "Do you give new people lists to work with or do you expect us to find our own leads right away? What are the commission splits for your average salespeople? Highest salespeople?"

Her interviewer looked surprised by her directness, took her questions seriously, and answered her thoroughly. While Diana was listening to him, she sent energy through her power center out into his office to leave a positive psychic imprint.

Two days after the meeting, the interviewer called Diana and offered her exactly the position she'd been looking for. Delighted, she almost accepted on the spot, but caught herself and asked him for a couple of days to think it over.

In the end, Diana realized that she did not feel comfortable in the real estate world. She decided it took too much of her psychic energy to look as if she fit in, and declined the offer. Here, too, however, she learned a valuable market lesson—he wanted to know which firm had "snapped her up" instead. Diana was pleased with her own psychic power success and vowed to use her tools more often.

⚛

In any meeting where you want a reaction from others, their psychic attunement is more important than yours.

⚛

The main mistake we make in dealing with other people is trying to communicate with them without forging a psychic connection. If you want to be heard and you want to move people to action, you have to speak their language. Diana used psychic "context clues" to figure out what, above all, was important to her interviewer (money and sales) and employed her third eye to focus on what he needed to hear, even if his questions weren't verbally forthright.

The case for psychic attunement is particularly relevant not only to interviewing but also in circumstances where you won't have the opportunity to identify people's astrological sign or analyze their handwriting. You're always meeting new people in normal business situations, and you'll find that using power tools to get an "inner handle" on how they work and think will make all the diffence in the world. You can sense whether they are political, malicious, truthful, diffident, dedicated, or loyal, all of which certainly help or hinder the various goings-on of business. Even when you know people already, psychic attunement can help you discern what's going on with them on a regular basis.

Body language, the most commonly accepted tip-off to someone's state of mind, is also a psychic power tool. It is always a psychic challenge to get someone to uncross his or her arms to open up to you! The following tips on countering anxiety, anger, and distraction will prove useful in those situations where you need to break through one's psychic scanner, particularly when you're selling something (whether it's a car or an idea), buying something (like a computer or even a company), or simply trying to get a group to come up with new ideas.

Anxiety

If people are obviously anxious about something, they need to feel that you aren't adding to their anxiety. Send them support through your heart center. To make the most of your meeting, send them blue energy from your throat into theirs, then visualize it coming back to you. This circle of energy can add the clarity that is often lacking when someone is ill at ease.

Anger

If your boss, client, or equivalent is upset about something you said, did, or didn't do, immediately surround yourself with white or pink light. It doesn't matter what color you choose, really, just visualize a protective cloud of light around you so you don't end up absorbing their negativity. Once you are protected, you're able to react appropriately and not defensively.

If you are in the wrong, own up to it while sending heart energy in the direction of your accuser. This will reinforce your regret and sincerity.

If you are being falsely accused, send energy from your throat center for clarity, state that which is untrue, and sit back quietly. If the opportunity presents itself, use your third eye to search for whoever is really responsible for the problem. Do not push back but do cover your power center. There is no reason to engage in a battle, particularly in business, unless you are being threatened. Calm denial is often more convincing than strong indignation.

And whatever you do, leave the room if the energy gets too aggressive. There is no winning with people who are out of control. If you are in a restrictive setting, be it physical like an airplane, or mental like a meeting, excuse yourself and ask for help, if you need it, in order to extricate yourself from the situation. There is no excuse for sitting still for abuse unless you are being held against your will.

Distraction

Sometimes you just can't get away even when you know the person you are meeting with is in no shape to concentrate. When you have to stay put and deal with someone else's messy or unfocused energy, you can ease the situation by sending him or her energy from your different psychic centers.

If people are spacing out while you're trying to converse with them, place your hand on them just long enough to send root energy through your hand into their body. You can make a simple gesture, like touching a shoulder or arm when you are making a point. If you're prepared, you can ground them in just a split second.

To do this, plant your feet firmly on the ground. Visualize that you are pulling earth energy up into your root and sending it from there into your hands. You can do this in a quick moment—you won't have to miss a beat of conversation and your words will be that much more focused and productive.

Reading Psychic Impressions

Tuning in to people can definitely give you an enormous amount of insight about who they are and how they work.

When you meet with a person who is saying one thing but psychically sending a totally different signal—like the old Marx Brothers routine, "Hello, I must be going"—your psychic power tools will give you the edge to know what's really going on. For instance, I happened to have a meeting scheduled once with an executive, and just before it he was told that he had to come up with a huge report in less than two days. He was flustered but he didn't want me to know it. While he said, "No, no, please let's have our meeting," his psychic energy said, "Get out of my way, I have to work!"

I didn't want to continue with our meeting as scheduled because I knew it would be unproductive. In order to spare his dignity, I claimed it was a bad time for me, too. I called him back after his deadline and he thanked me for being so understanding and offered to pay me for my time.

You can practice using your third eye to "see" your audience or you can try some other techniques: using the crown, the solar plexus or the human touch. You might be surprised by how much you can learn using these methods.

Psychic Receptor	What It Feels Like
Crown	All of a sudden, I just knew it.
Third eye	I saw it happen before it actually did.
Power center/Navel center	I felt it in my bones.

You can get information through your crown center just like a bolt of lightning (there's that lightbulb going off again). This happens to me pretty frequently; when I was in advertising I used to get teased about it. I recall a meeting in which a team of us were wrestling over which of two strategies to use to advertise our product, a new toy. There were equally compelling arguments on both sides, but there in the meeting, I just knew that one strategy would work better than the other. It was a more competitive approach rather than one in which the toy was simply featured for its attractive benefits. I told my clients that I'd heard via the grapevine that there was going to be a real war in this market and that we'd best take the competition out quickly. (Okay, I stretched the truth here, but I didn't lie—I "heard" it through the psychic grapevine.) Because there was no real reason not to pursue this strategy, we developed the advertising campaign based on this competitive stance and the head of the toy company loved it. At Christmastime, when the advertising really hit hard, our product sold the best in a crowded category.

My friend Sherry is always telling me that she "sees" things in the shower, and being less inhibited than most, she freely goes to her job as a high-profile market analyst and shares her shower visions with her coworkers. As her track record is excellent, they listen with great interest. She also "sees" unconsciously when she is conversing, sometimes getting information while she is in the middle of a meeting. You can always tell when people are getting information because they stop, stare off into the distance for a second, and lose their focus. Then, just as suddenly, they're back, often hastening to jot the new idea down. This is common, so don't be perplexed if it happens to you—and be sure to take the mindstorm seriously.

My client Albert gets his feelings by touching someone on the shoulder or wrist. He's very careful, though. When he meets a new person he always shakes hands in order to make this physical connection—and he tells me that his gut reaction is "always right." After our first handshake, he told me I was an exceptionally astute person; I'd say he probably does have good "gut" instincts!

Most of us use only one kind of psychic "hearing," not because we're not capable of others, but because we favor one. If you don't know which is your best psychic receiving center, just practice with each one until you find the one that works best. And believe me—you'll know it when you find it. After some practice, you'll realize that you automatically read people when you really want to know more about them. Psychic techniques often become automatic reactions, and you won't even notice how easily you'll respond. I'm so used to tuning in to other people that I often end up knowing more about them than I want to. If that happens to you, simply put your hand on your forehead to tune out!

PSYCHIC POWER TOOLS AND TECHNIQUES FOR GROUPS

When you're faced with addressing a group of people, no matter how large or small, you can use your power tools to improve your performance and put the audience at ease. If possible, try this three-tiered approach:

1. Set up a psychically receptive room.
2. Psych yourself up.
3. Create a psychic rapport with your audience.

Your Psychic Reception Room

You don't *have* to get into the conference room or office beforehand, but it sure helps. Just a few sprinkles of specific herbs here and there, some flowers, and maybe a power object like a crystal or stone, and you can shift the atmosphere of the most dreary room into a far more receptive space. You can also stack the deck in your favor if you raise the elemental energy in the room; it keeps people awake and can make you feel much more comfortable.

One of my clients, Gwen, was both excited and anxious about giving a potentially career-making presentation. At my insistence, she arranged to get into the room to rehearse with her slides and to practice at the podium beforehand, and brought a few extras with her.

In the corners of the large boardroom, Gwen placed small sprigs of lavender, knowing it would make the crowd more relaxed and receptive. A secret power tool, the herb was virtually undetectable on the carpeted floor. Next, she placed two big vases of carnations on the table to amplify the room's energy. Then she set a few small, inconspicuous crystals—she chose jade for grounding—on each side of the room to bring in some elemental energy to hold the space. Finally, Gwen cleverly put an orange sweater she had no intention of wearing on the back of her chair to raise the aura of success around her.

Unlike my client Melissa's experience (described in the Preface), Gwen felt that the energy of the room was lively and upbeat, just how she wanted her crowd to feel. She wore a subdued dress in navy blue, and added an aquamarine pendant at her throat center to keep her speaking clear. She chose the scent of lavender rather than her usual fragrance to keep her calm and to match the energy of the room.

As she spoke, Gwen felt her power and heart centers humming. Talk about really "being" in the moment! She felt strong, confident, prepared, and secure, knowing she'd left no psychic stone unturned. As a result, her physical presentation was flawless, and despite her concerns, her audience was interested in and supportive of her ideas. Unaware of any telltale signs of psychic manipulation, the group simply sensed that Gwen was intelligent and articulate, and was extremely receptive to her. After the meeting, Gwen received compliments and congratulations from her colleagues who had heard from others how well it had gone.

Power Tools for Presentations

You are already acquainted with the basic power tools from chapter 2; psychic power tools for meetings and presentations are merely an extension of these. For example, you probably don't want to put a picture of your power animal up in the conference room, but you can use a tool like a power animal in more subtle ways. You can also do as Gwen did, and create a good psychic energy in the room using flowers and herbs, and then "hold the space" with stones or crystals. You'll be relieved to know that there is no need to call attention to these power preparations; the use of your personal tools does not require permission or public announcement.

Power from Flowers and Herbs

You can apply power tools to a presentation room without being too aggressive about it, just as Gwen did. Find the herbs that are associated with the properties you want to manifest or use those that play down certain energies, if that's the desired effect. Consult the list of power herbs (pages 43–44) for some ideas.

When you place the herbs in a room, don't be concerned with quantity. It isn't a matter of how much you use; even just a few petals or bits will do. What makes all the difference to your success is your intention. Try to place your intention in the room as you sprinkle the substance around.

For instance, if you want your audience to remain calm, relaxed, and reasonable while you reveal unpleasant or challenging news, sprinkle some lavender around, and while doing so, send soothing energy into the room. You can do this by breathing through your heart center. You can also do what the great magic workers did back in the old days; enchant your space.

Enchantment is simply adding the element of sound to your task, so you "chant" power into the room. I don't mean that you should sing solo as you fling your herbs into the corners of the room; I mean simply saying aloud, "Here's some lavender to keep everyone relaxed." That's all. No big deal. I did this many times, often to the delight of my coworkers, who wanted to know more about enchantments. If you can't bring yourself to say something out loud, that's okay—at least breathe the intention of the herb as you place it. When you exhale naturally, send the intention of the herb out to the room.

Herbs, flowers, gems, and stones will work on their own.

The only reason you should consider the use of enchantments is to keep your intention on top of your mind. It is so easy to get distracted before a big presentation that you may find yourself thinking about something else while you're setting up your psychically receptive room, which lessens the power of your preparations.

Flowers work well to dispel anxiety and open our centers of compassion and joy. Just pick the right mix for your occasion, or if you don't have control over what is chosen, use herbs to enhance or counter the flower power.

POWERS FROM FLOWERS

Chrysanthemum	Protection from evil
Camellia	Riches
Carnation	Power
Daffodil	Rebirth, hopefulness
Holly	Protection
Iris	Faith, wisdom, and valor
Lily (white)	Protection
Lily (tiger; orange)	Power
Lily of the valley	Mental agility
Orchid	Enhanced intuition
Rose (pink)	Friendliness
Rose (white)	Protection
Rose (yellow)	Power, success
Snapdragon	Protection
Sunflower	Success, wisdom
Tulip	Safeguard against bad luck

HERBS FOR MEETINGS

In addition to those herbs introduced in chapter 2, these may help you with a successful public appearance, be it one-on-one or in front of a large auditorium full of people:

FOR COURAGE

Borage
Sweetpea
Tea
Yarrow

FOR PEACE AND HARMONY AMONG THE GROUP

Gardenia
Lavender
Olive
Passionflower
Vervain
Violet

FOR SUCCESS IN LEGAL MATTERS

Hickory
Marigold

TO MANIFEST WISHES

Bamboo
Dandelion
Dogwood
Ginseng
Sage
Walnut

Holding the Space

Holding a space is a way of anchoring the psychic atmosphere you create, so that the energy of success or relaxation you've imprinted or the power zap you've given a room won't be lost before you've started your meeting. Anchoring keeps the room or space connected to your energy, and most important, safe from the toxicity of others. It would take a lot of disruption and negativity to change your atmosphere when you hold your space.

You hold your space with any kind of power object, but in my experience and that of my clients, the most effective method is to use representations of the elements. By placing small stones or objects representing each element near each wall in the presentation room, you will fix your atmosphere until you're finished with it. You are basically assigning an element (fire, earth, air, or water) to each direction, and by doing so you create a kind of psychic force field. You don't need to be concerned about which element is best for each direction; there are varying opinions and no right answer. I have such a bad sense of direction that I probably get it wrong even when I try, and the technique has never failed me. Just place a representation of each element in the direction of your choice. The point is to have each element equally present in the room.

⊗

There is one general rule for selecting a crystal or stone to represent an element: Use its color to guide you.

⊗

White is water; blue and purple are air; brown and green are earth; and red, yellow, and orange are fire. If you can't find something in those colors, use your instincts. I've often used stones or shells I found at the beach for water. A feather satisfies air, and any token of nature that comes from the land will fill in for earth, like acorns, pinecones, leaves, or twigs. The fire element is harder to substitute, but there are so many stones you can use, you shouldn't have to look any further.

CRYSTALS, STONES, AND OBJECTS TO HOLD A SPACE

Assign one wall to each element and put one object representing that element against the wall.

Fire	Tigereye, red agate, jasper, ruby, garnet, yellow peridot, citrine, bloodstone
Earth	Jade, emerald, malachite, acorns, pinecones, twigs, rocks, flowers, plants
Air	Lapis lazuli, sapphire, aquamarine, turquoise, blue topaz, amethyst, feathers
Water	Moonstone, opal, rose quartz, shells, stones from rivers or seas

Psychic Room Preparation from Afar

As you know, there are many times when you can't get into a room before you're on. In this case, you can do a few psychic preparations from afar to get the energy going, but it becomes increasingly difficult if your presentation is preceded by others. Consider a stand-up comic trying to control the atmosphere of a nightclub; you've heard the expression "he's a tough act to follow"—it's nearly impossible to alter the crowd's mood after four other comics have already influenced it. If you present after someone who was boring, you'll have to pep them up. If the preceding presenter was dynamic, you'll have to find a way to be even better.

You can take a few steps to prepare before you're in the hot seat. Using your psychic energy centers, you can send your power ahead of you. To your advantage, you can do this well before the event, from anywhere, and it will still be effective. You can also anchor the energy you create by carrying power objects with you.

For example, a client of mine is a scientist, and he was leaving to give a talk at a university in another state. He was very uncomfortable speaking in front of large groups and asked if I could help him relax. I told him to find an object that represented stability for him, and he chose a pair of cuff links his grandfather had given him. Coincidentally, they had small jade insets, excellent for grounding.

Before he even entered the room, he tried the following exercise while holding his jade cuff links.

SENDING YOUR POWER AHEAD OF YOU

Find an object that embodies how you want to feel at your event. Hold it in your hand during this exercise.

Sit quietly, allowing your breathing to relax. Feel your power center at your solar plexus. Open it with yellow energy gliding in and out, back to front and front to back. Feel sunlight emanating from this center.

Feel your third eye. See purple light flowing in and out of it. See yourself, speaking, presenting, or just being accepted by people who are listening to you.

Shine the light coming from your power center into the space where your audience is. Feel their receptiveness. Visualize your success. You are completely at ease. Your power center glows with energy.

Sit with this vision and this energy until you feel complete with it. Before you let it go, blow it into the future. Use your breath to gently send your vision and its feeling into the day and time and space on which you need it. Know that your power will meet you there. As you blow your vision into the future, touch or squeeze your power object, knowing that your vision is anchored within it.

When you are finished, open your eyes and put your hands firmly on the ground. You have just straddled your energy into the future, and you need to ground yourself back to the present. Allow yourself a few moments to gather yourself after the exercise.

My somewhat reluctant scientist client did do this exercise, and couldn't wait to tell me how it worked out. It seems he was perfectly at ease in his talk, a first for him. He added that he didn't even flinch when the projectionist didn't show his slides properly. He was able to joke around with his audience even when his key results were flashed upside down.

My client, like many people, suffers not only from a dislike of public speaking but also from stage fright. This exercise can also help you calm down if you get nervous. The sensation of butterflies in the stomach is an indication of a flickering and unstable power center.

The same exercise can help you with other public speaking ailments. Just add the appropriate energy center to the exercise. Here are a few examples:

Presentation Ailment	Power Center
Speaking too long	Throat, crown
"Ums"	Throat
Shifting around	Root
Speaking too fast	Heart
Stage fright	Heart
Sweaty palms	Solar plexus
Butterflies	Solar plexus
Tight throat	Throat
Thin voice	Throat
Dry mouth	Throat
Freezing on the spot	Root

Anchor Objects

Make sure that you choose an object that correlates with the exercise. I have one client who keeps a stopwatch in his pocket to anchor time, because his tendency is to go on too long. Any grounding herbs (flower petals, seeds) or crystals (agate or jasper) will help you stay on your feet without shifting back and forth as well as keep you from speaking too fast. Clarity crystals (any quartz) or herbs (rosemary, spearmint) will work on those "ums." I've used a stick of Wrigley's spearmint in a pinch for an anchor before a big presentation! You can always choose something that holds the right sentiment, whether or not it's a crystal, herb, or power object. As long as it is made of substantially natural materials, it can work for you.

For Your Future Needs

The above exercise can be used beyond public speaking. In fact, you're already unconsciously sending your energy into the future when you look forward to (or dread) an event. Your psychic power tools and skills can work ahead of you to create the atmosphere and reception you want.

Use it for entertaining, conventions, office parties, any situation in which you want to feel more comfortable. Be sure not to forget your power object; it anchors both the feeling and the event to you.

For negotiating a deal, send your energy from the throat center (blue) combined with energy from the power center (yellow). This will ease your part of the conversation and add to the power of your side. Wear something red, as it communicates passion and affords protection.

If you are trying to buy something, anchor an object that represents magnetism (a real magnet or lodestone is excellent), wear an outfit that both welcomes and enhances trust (wool or cotton with blues or purples), and carry a grounding stone.

If you are selling something, increase the desirability of your product by anointing it with an actual power scent (if possible) or by creating a charm with the product's name written inside it. Choose an outfit in cotton, a neutral color to disguise any leanings you might have, and send energy from your solar plexus into the future meeting.

For attracting opportunities, send your energy from your solar plexus to create your power presence and from your third eye to send "attractive" energy into the future. You may want to carry a charm that attracts success or an amulet made of a magnet or lodestone with your astrological sign or your name written on it. Keep a basket or wreath of pinecones—or a vase of honeysuckle—in your office, both of which hasten good fortune. Don't limit yourself colorwise; you'll want to be open to every opportunity in every moment.

For maximizing the quality of what you are sending out, I recommend sitting with your project or letter or whatever you are sending out and putting energy into it before it hits the mailbox. Send energy from your heart center into the future to clear the path for your project, to establish a connection between you and the person who will receive it. You can pass a crystal over the project to increase its power—try an emerald or sapphire—after all, you'll want it to be received as a jewel. Bless what you are sending out either aloud or with your exhaling breath.

To ward off negativity, use your clearing techniques with burning sage and sea salt. Send your energy into the future from all of your power centers, but do not do so until you've smudged yourself or have taken a salt shower. If you are trying to protect a certain project, write what you are trying to protect on a piece of paper. Sprinkle salt over it, then blow the salt off of it, into the wastebasket or out of the window. Deflect negativity from clients or colleagues by keeping a cube made of onyx in your office or on your person—the cube represents stability and groundedness, while the onyx absorbs negativity.

ENERGY AND ENTHUSIASM
Too Much

If you're at all like me, anticipation can just about kill any real enjoyment of an actual event. Like a child looking forward to a birthday party so much that he is cranky by the time it comes, some of us go into psychic overdrive just thinking about an upcoming date.

Calm down.

When you get overexcited in anticipation of something, you can miss a lot of important clues (you're being distracted). You might also run out of steam by the time the event comes along.

Krista, an executive who was receiving a sales achievement award at a national convention, was so much looking forward to her time to shine that she became too distracted to do her work. By putting off her sales reports and not attending to some minor shipping problems, she indirectedly created a major stink, all because she couldn't summon up enough work energy. By the time she received her award, some of her accounts were furious with her and her sales manager had to admonish her the day before the ceremony. Needless to say, her pride burst quickly when she realized her orders for the current month were her worst ever.

You don't have to fall into that pattern. Just allow yourself to send your energy into the future with the previous exercise, then let it rest. If you find that you can't stop thinking about the upcoming event, keep your power object with you and give it a squeeze now and then. You will also benefit from grounding yourself. Consult the earth-amplifying exercise in chapter 4 (page 117).

Too Little

If you're simply not into the event as it comes closer, you could say that your "heart isn't in it" and you'd be right, at least on a psychic level. When your psychic energy becomes slow, tired, or numb around something you originally believed in or held dear, your heart connection has waned.

My client Richard was to attend a convention of agricultural engineers where he was a keynote speaker. In his organization, being a speaker on the dais of the opening dinner was the highest honor bestowed, but the agricultural engineers had asked Richard to speak at the breakfast the following morning. He felt that he had been undervalued and overlooked. (Richard, by the way, is a Leo, and naturally loves the limelight.)

He grumbled and grumped for weeks before the convention, rather than paying attention to writing his speech. By the time he got around to it, his mood had tainted his remarks to the point that his speech sounded sarcastic and sharp. He attended the welcoming dinner and saw that although the speakers were certainly industry leaders, attendance was very low that evening. Taking some satisfaction in that, he sauntered back into the hall for his breakfast the next day without any nervousness. Upon arriving, he realized that the hall was now fully attended and that those very people who spoke the evening before were sitting right under his nose! He quickly realized he had misjudged the importance they were giving his speech, and with little time to spare, kept his head and left the hall. He had fifteen minutes before he was to speak.

In that fifteen minutes, he held his success amulet tightly, softened up his speech by focusing on his heart center (although he kept some sharp humor in so that he could "wake up" his audience), and breathed clarity and calm into his throat center and third eye. He then took the podium as if facing a board of inquiry and allowed his speech to flow with some ad libbed comments. The speech was received well and Richard was congratulated, but he confided to me later that he could have done so much better "if only he had known." Richard was his own worst enemy in his lack of enthusiasm.

This lackluster feeling can come from many causes, not just wounded pride. Fear, of course, is a leading factor. You could be unconsciously afraid of the event itself because you might fail, yes, but you also might succeed. Or you may just dread its anticlimax I tend to get glum on the day of an event because the great day has finally arrived and it will quickly come to an end.

Being cool around an important event is a way of controlling overexcitement, but it can also contain the very energy you need to create a success.

Regardless of the cause of your dullness, you need to reconnect with the heart of the matter. If you can't find the energy to do that, use the fire-amplifying exercise in chapter 4 (page 116) to give you a jump start.

REVVING UP
YOUR LOST ENTHUSIASM

Sit quietly with a representation of the subject of your lost enthusiasm. Close your eyes and go back in time to when you were excited about it, when you believed in it. It may be when you first started working with it, or even just yesterday. Stay with that time. Breathe it in. Feel its possibilities and success. Send your heart energy into the vision. Surround it with green light. Breathe this light back into your heart, taking with it the feeling and vision of belief and hope. Sit with the vision in your heart. See how you feel. Peaceful? Uncomfortable? Hopeful? Fearful? Now breathe space into your feelings, allowing yourself to feel light, open to all possibilities. Know that your energy is even and open. When you feel complete, open your eyes and ground yourself by putting your hands on the floor.

BORROWING INTEREST: USING SOMEONE ELSE'S ENTHUSIASM

Find people who are excited about the subject at hand, perhaps even friends who have nothing to do with your work or your project. Ask them individually what good they see in it. As they tell you what they think, do not "edit" or contradict them. Don't even listen if you don't want to. Just breathe their energy into your heart. Try to inhale their words and enthusiasm. Take in the light and the sparks of passion that fly out when they speak. Encourage them to talk more, adding more ideas and excitement to the discussion. Keep breathing their energy into your heart. When they are finished talking, thank them and leave the subject. Do not discuss your own views and do not criticize their input. If you feel comfortable, ask them for a penny or a little object you can carry with you.

Their energy will now integrate with your own and you'll find you are more open to more positive possibilities.

ENDINGS: FIRINGS AND FAREWELLS

It is just as important to know how to say good-bye for the last time as it is to say hello for the first time. We as a society are excellent at neglecting this area, and we pay for it dearly. Whether you choose—or you are asked—to leave a place, a job, or an office, psychic closure will leave others with a positive psychic impression, and more important, keep you fresh and ready to psychically impress those you'll meet at your next stop.

When You Leave

When you take final leave of a place, you are taking your energy away from it. Obviously, your physical being won't be there, but you can easily and unintentionally leave behind emotional and psychic impressions. I call this a dirty departure. Why does this matter? Because although you may think it's okay to leave a little of yourself behind, you are also keeping a bit of the place you are leaving with you. In instances of employment, the best thing to take is your experience, your contacts, and your memories; nothing more. Unless you're wise and act accordingly, you could end up hauling a lot of baggage with you—which can seriously weigh you down.

If you've ever heard someone talking incessantly about their old job, their last office, or constantly using the phrase "we used to" this and "we used to" that, they are dragging behind the past like an old ball and chain. You can't live productively in the present or create the future when you're constantly quoting the past. And the longer you've been in one place, the more important this process is.

Psychically, it is very easy to detach as long as you are emotionally at peace with your change. Don't leave in a huff, in a hurry, or thinking that paradise is lost forever. Try to get a new perspective on the situation and visualize how you would like to change it or re-create it next.

An imprint of your psychic energy will be left behind, but it's only a temporary impression that lasts as long as the work you did is still ongoing and as long as you are remembered. Even a temporary secretary can make a psychic impression on the place that lasts for a long while. It simply depends on you.

The easiest way to avoid a dirty departure is to do two simple things before leaving:

1. Say good-bye and thanks out loud.
2. Hand over a symbol of your attachment. Consider handing over a company key chain, your nameplate, even just the bathroom key. This is a symbolic relinquishment of your attachment to the place and creates psychic closure. You won't carry psychic residue with you and you'll be clear to start your next job.

By not achieving closure, you're staying psychically attached, which can make your energy centers sluggish in new situations and can prevent you from acclimating your new job.

Good-byes

If you are so lucky as to have a going-away party, you have a convenient place to graciously thank those around you. Simple but powerful.

In the more common scenario of just leaving, try to have face-to-face contact with your superior and your close associates.

When you are leaving a bad situation, if you can't squeak out words of gratitude, just say good-bye with a neutral energy. Don't carry on with hostility, or you are dirtying up things and possibly burning (real or karmic) bridges. You don't need to "get even" now; you need to cleanse yourself and release the experience.

Saying good-bye not only makes it real, it helps to cut the psychic ties to the past. Like a breakup of a love affair, there can be emotional kickbacks, sadness, and even tears, especially if leaving is a rite of passage or you don't want to go. Remember, mourning is natural (remember the famous *Mary Tyler Moore Show* farewell scene) and it's important to your physical, psychological, and mental health to release sad feelings.

Handovers

Like a mayor handing over the keys of a city, you can ceremoniously relinquish your hold on a place. Literally hand over keys to someone else, or pass on your computer mouse, or your ID card. To do this with a psychic spin, simply add more ceremony by articulating what you are doing. As you relinquish your last ties to your job, add psychic intention to it and say:

"I hand you these keys and say good-bye to this place."

"I hereby relinquish my bathroom key and take my leave."

Or, at the very least:

"I'm outta here!"

Being Let Go: The Darker Side of Good-byes

Don't fret. It happens to everyone. For whatever reason, your fate is taking you elsewhere, and whether or not you are delighted to start afresh or trembling with anger or fear, use your power tools to let you glide out gracefully.

Even if you've known your job was going to be terminated, the news can still cause quite a shock. Reality always packs a bigger punch than probabilities. Just remember, you lost your job, not your power. You can take your talent somewhere more compatible with your energy.

You have to add only a few steps to the basic good-bye instructions to help you ease out the door without psychic power loss.

1. Get the anger, fear, or sadness out in private, not in the office. Once you are let go, you are a lame duck. You don't have to go in at all if you don't want to.
2. Take a salt shower or bath before going in for the last day or week.
3. Use your power center constantly, and cover it whenever anyone you don't like approaches. Don't use it for aggressive behavior; you'll lose more than you gain.
4. Stay away from sympathy givers. They'll dump toxic rubbish all over you; you're not to be pitied.

After you've been handed your walking papers, you do not owe your soon-to-be former employer any honest emotion.

Don't bother, even if you like them a lot. You need to evoke a protective shielding so that you don't give away too much of your energy and so that you don't take on any of theirs. This is a breakup, not of affections, but of power sharing. You are best off cutting the cord quickly and efficiently so you don't bleed your power away.

For those of you who are furious or feel unjustly dismissed, read chapter 7's various suggestions for safe psychic revenge.

❧ 7 ❧

PSYCHIC POWER
AND OTHER PEOPLE:

The Dark Side

There is no escaping the fact that bad things happen once in a while—to everyone. There are times when you're going to be cheated, taken advantage of, or rejected, and you might not find it in your heart to forgive and forget so easily. You may not be able to avoid unpleasantness altogether, but with psychic power tools, you do have control over how you deal with it.

So what can you do? You can learn a few simple tricks to turn the psychic tide back in your favor—and, if you insist, you can seek safe (but satisfying) psychic revenge on your offender. You can also protect yourself from being a target for someone else's karmic mess.

PETTY POWER PLAYERS

There are many corporate animals out there who think that classic "power" behavior will make them powerful. As if eating raw meat, drinking lots of booze, or driving a chauffeured car is powerful stuff. This behavior is fine if you really enjoy it, but doing it to convince others that you're a "player" just won't work.

I once worked with an organization where the president loved to drink vodka and play golf. In order to succeed, most of his executive staff tried to emulate him. One executive, a Mormon, did not. He was a committed family man, never drank, and didn't care much for golf. His career was in good shape, and in spite of the fact that he didn't behave like the rest of the good ol' boys, he ended up on a fast track, passing some of the president's drinking buddies because of his performance and self-assuredness.

There is nothing wrong with hanging out socially with the boss or with your coworkers, but don't bother doing it just for political reasons. If you're being disingenuous, you'll be doing yourself more harm than good—and you won't be able to access your psychic power clearly. Posturing saps energy.

Petty power players often favor outdated, almost trite, tactics to make themselves feel superior to others. Here are a few. In some cases, you won't need your psychic power as much as you'll need your common sense to sidestep these tricksters.

The Early Bird

Early birds consistently get in much earlier than their colleagues for no real reason, and make sure everyone knows it. My hunch is that they do this to look more dedicated than their colleagues. I once visited an office where there was an unofficial contest to see who would come in the earliest—one guy had actually come to work at 3:30 A.M. The runner-up was there at 4:00 A.M.

If you are irritated by grandstanding of this nature and don't want to participate in petty power plays, just use a little common sense. Try one of these lines out on your overzealous coworker, spiked with a little kick from your power center.

"Got kicked out of the house?"

"Too bad you're so behind in your work."

"Gosh, didn't you finish that thing yet?"

You get the picture. Turn the situation around to show the disempowering nature of their tactic, then move on. But don't spend too much time on them or you'll actually be feeding their power.

Late for Nothings

One of the most aggravating and unprofessional things people can do is waste your time. Being late for meetings is a common petty power play.

You know the drill. You're waiting in a conference room or at a lunch table or even on a street corner, and the person you are meeting arrives ten, fifteen, or even thirty minutes late.

You have to trust your intuition to know if people have kept you waiting for a genuine reason (their car has broken down, they were caught in another meeting without a phone, and so on) or if they're just trying to look more important by being so busy—and so late. If you are waiting outside their office and you can tell they're on the phone gassing with a friend, they are clearly petty power players.

Here's what to do the next time this happens to you. Take no notice of their apology (if there is one) or how late they actually are, and override it with pity. Pity is an extremely hostile emotion (allowing you to look down at someone else's misfortune) and can one-up the petty power player rather neatly. Petty power players are not interested in martyrdom; they want to be thought of as heavily in demand.

Cover your power center while they're saying how sorry they are for being late, and uncover it when you respond. Send energy from your third eye into their third eye with the message "I know that you are lying and I do not cater to this kind of behavior." If you can squeeze your power amulet or charm simultaneously you'll get a good zap going.

In response to their apology, allow yourself to be a little patronizing while sending energy through your power center. Say:

"Oh, I'm so sorry you're so overburdened. They're obviously not being very good to you."

"It's such a shame they work you so hard. I guess they just undervalue you."

"You know, I heard about this great book on coping with stress—maybe I should send you a copy?"

Nasty, isn't it? I can guarantee you, they won't want to hear much more of that, and your not-so-sincere sympathy will prompt a quick time change for the next meeting.

You could also say nothing. Responding to an effusive (but disingenuous) apology with silence can also be very effective. My most memorable experience of this occurred when I was the offender, a very junior account executive who kept a very senior magazine rep waiting. After I finished yakking on the phone to a friend, the gentleman finally came into my office, took his coat off leisurely, sat down, and smiled. He didn't say a word, forcing me, flustered, to blab on for at least five minutes with an apology. I've never felt so foolish in my life.

Proximity Players

I think any kind of bold butt-kissing is abhorrent, but there are plenty of people out there who do it. My old advertising buddy, Hank, used to call them "bag carriers." They're the corporate equivalent of the teacher's pet, the people who always have to sit next to the boss or next to the most important person in the room. They're the kind who measure power by the square footage of your office and its proximity to the boss's office.

Proximity players tend to start or disseminate rumors and other corporate conspiracies and often get overexcited about dull details, like who's moving to what office and how many windows it has. Don't get caught up in this; powerful people produce strong results wherever they sit. Protect yourself from psychic power struggles with brilliant diamond light energy and try not to associate with these types, even if their energy seems very magnetic.

Name-Droppers

Name-droppers use other people's perceived power to make themselves sound connected and important. Everyone drops a name now and then; it's hard not to in business. Yet people who drop names all the time clearly have nothing much to say for themselves.

If you can, simply walk away from a name-dropper. Otherwise, use your energy centers to increase the space between you and him. Smile politely and try to steer conversation in a more constructive direction. Send your third eye energy into his third eye—this will distract his focus and help you switch the subject. Take no notice of the names as they thud on the floor in front of you. You can always pretend not to know who the name-dropper is talking about, but be prepared to appear bored if he insists on explaining.

Petty Piggy Posturers

I can't help but laugh at the sight of power posturing, in part because it's the least powerful position to assume and because it's very unbecoming. Leaning back in your desk chair and raising your arms above your head, yawning as you talk, or sitting at a lunch meeting with poor table manners does not make for a powerful persona and certainly doesn't send positive body language.

Real power is a combination of being at ease with yourself and using common courtesy; lately, however, I see this mutation of power posturing taking on a more brutish form.

If you are subjected to corporate pig behavior, don't take it upon yourself to play Mommy or Daddy and correct it. From your power center, send a little "smack" of energy into his solar plexus. This often leads to some discomfort, which makes quite an impact but doesn't do any permanent damage. You can also send root energy into the ground, which will steady your power and anchor you as a force to be reckoned with.

I listened in deep admiration to a story one of my clients, Vonnie, told. Vonnie was asked to attend a small, select seminar on a new financial product her firm was offering. Most of the executives in attendance were men with at least twenty years of experience in the company, with the exception of a young investment banker who had earned a reputation as a maverick for putting together big, daring deals. This young man decided to sit next to my client in the seminar. During the first hour, he stretched, leaned, and yawned, showing his obvious lack of interest. At one point he closed his eyes, as if the seminar was too painful for him to watch. Vonnie took this opportunity to send him soothing psychic impressions through her third eye, as if she was singing him a lullaby. She surrounded him with an aura of pink light, also soothing to his energy. She hoped he would just relax and stop distracting her. Instead, he actually fell asleep—and snored. The entire seminar group stopped and focused on him. When they broke for lunch, he woke up and turned to look at Vonnie in a daze. She couldn't help but laugh. His associates call him "Sleepy" now, and he is no longer looked upon as such a maverick.

CHEATS, LIARS, AND OTHER CORPORATE CRIMINALS

Enough about petty offenders—it's time to go after the real villains. I am not talking about those white collar criminals who bilk us out of millions every year. Those people usually run into their karma by facing failure or illness—note Michael Milken's battle with prostate cancer, Ivan Boesky's jail sentence, or the many bankrupted robber barons of the eighties. It is far more productive (and gratifying) to concentrate on the creeps who mess with your success, usurp your opportunities, or outright lie to you for no discernible reason. I'm talking about bosses who say you're doing a terrific job when they're already looking for your replacement—or supervisors who say you'll be promoted in six months, every six months, just to pass you up again. Or colleagues who overhear you telling a friend about a great idea, only to take it for their own.

Before you can move on to psychic revenge techniques, I have to ask you to do something unpleasant. I have to ask you to look at the situation and figure out what *you* had to do with it. Are you at all responsible for your part in being misled? Some of the time, the answer is yes, like when "it sounded too good to be true but . . ." or you simply wanted to believe "it was all for the best." Did you allow your intuition a chance to voice its opinion? Certainly not. Every time someone else got promoted—did you watch, letting yourself be coddled into believing you'd get one, too, just because you didn't want to make a stink or leave the company?

Here's the thing: Don't believe everything you're told. Because no one can force you to do anything you don't want to do, you are, in most cases, responsible in part for allowing someone else to get the better of you. You might have even given them the power to do so.

My friend Karla really wanted to believe the job description she'd been given at an employment agency (it was great) but found in reality that the job was little more than being an administrative assistant. She'd been told that she would screen people, prep them for interviews, and use the knowledge she had acquired with her human resources major in business school. What greater experience for a recent grad than helping place people in jobs? Answer: real-world experience in deciphering misleading want ads and unscrupulous hiring techniques. This was a first-class lesson in how the real world worked, but Karla was furious that she fell for it.

Karla had to move on, both from her job and from her feeling of being taken advantage of. She might have simply moved on and repeated the pattern, but the worst she could do was to stay. Then she'd be responsible for going nowhere.

Lying and cheating can be contagious behavior when you don't deal with it. If you find yourself muttering any of these phrases, you're headed in the wrong direction.

"If it worked for them, it'll work for me."

"If you can't beat 'em, join 'em."

"It's just the way things are done."

"I had to go through it and I lived."

If you're trying to justify being less than honest or upright about your moves, you're going to have to face karmic justice. I suggest you reconsider your tactics.

All-Purpose Revenge: A Psychic Mirror

Here's a way to safely send nasty old energy back where it came from. It's called creating a psychic mirror—it literally reflects people's negativity right back at them.

I once had an office next to one of the most toxic people I have ever met. No matter how nicely anybody behaved toward him, he was rude, insulting, and unfortunately, untouchable, because he was the founding partner's nephew. He wielded his influence with pride and made a target of me, his only bordering neighbor. He listened in on my phone conversations, made comments to others about my appearance, and speculated loudly about my social life.

I successfully employed a large-scale psychic mirror, and almost immediately, things took a turn for the better. He seemed to lose interest in my phone calls, he stopped appraising my appearance and giving me lewd looks, and even when I had to speak to him about business, he wasn't as rude as he had been in the past.

Here are three psychic mirror exercises for specific causes. You can make your own up for other situations once you get the gist of these. A purse-size mirror is easiest to use. You're apt to get one as a promotion in the mail one day—keep it in your desk, even if it seems silly. It can be extremely useful.

LARGE-SCALE PSYCHIC MIRROR

For this exercise, you need a mirror, a flame (a match or lighter will do), some salt, and a glass of water.

Sit quietly and open your energy centers, starting with the root and opening to the crown. Feel your clarity, calm your breathing.

When you feel quiet, light your match. Make a clockwise circle with the flame. Blow it out. Pick up the salt. Sprinkle it in the four directions. In each direction, blow through your mouth as if you were blowing something away. Take your water and sprinkle it in the four directions.

Take your mirror in hand. Hold it up in each of the four directions and say, "I send back the negativity to its source." Say it each time you hold the mirror up.

Set the mirror down. Visualize the person in question gazing into a mirror and experience the pain he or she caused you.

You are now free of negative influence.

It is best not to look into the mirror again. Place it on a windowsill facing out to the world or facing the direction of the person in question. It need not be out in plain sight. Once you feel you've completed your psychic clearing, wash the mirror with salt water before using it for other purposes.

PSYCHIC MIRROR TO WARD OFF EVIL

If you're worried about people putting a curse on you (you'd be surprised how many people are) this works well. It also helps to alleviate anxiety while you sleep.

Place any size mirror next to your bed facing away from you, toward a window if possible. Sleep with the mirror in that position. Rinse the mirror with salt water before looking into it.

PSYCHIC MIRROR FOR DAILY PROTECTION

If you are subjected to negative energy in strong doses on a daily basis, try this technique. It works like a Saint Anthony medal.

Rig a little mirror onto a chain and wear it under your clothing against your power center or your heart center. This will keep you from absorbing any psychic energy at all—negative or supportive. An empty locket can work in place of a mirror if you clear it first and if it is highly polished. You literally need a reflection of light.

PSYCHIC CLEANSING FROM LYIN', CHEATIN' CROOKS

This is one of the hardest things you can do, and if you really do it well, you'll be going to heaven on the express train. The only way to sock it to lyin', cheatin' crooks is to reach into your heart and hand over some big fat forgiveness, in the form of truth-telling and serenity.

Liars and cheats operate in a realm where there isn't enough (goodness/money/stuff) to go around, and where they fear being found out for being a fraud (if they knew what they needed to know, they wouldn't have to cheat). Show them how little you fear them, how much you know, and you will own them. Karla ended up going into her bosses and telling them off for their misleading job description. Of course, she did this when she was handing in her resignation and was already miles past caring what they thought. They were more upset because Karla was going to work for a firm that had given them business (this is karmic justice the way we really like it).

It's possible you won't want to confront the liar/cheat at all. That's perfectly understandable, particularly if the person is likely to get very disturbed or violent when forced to confront the truth. In that case, you can do the exercise psychically. It will still work.

EXERCISE FOR RELEASING THE LIAR, CHEATER, OR CROOK

Imagine these people—have their picture or draw a crude picture, just for this purpose.

Light a white candle. Have a glass of drinking water next to you.

Imagine that you are surrounded with white light. Smudge your surroundings.

Surround their image with white light, even if you think they are full of dirty, evil energy. The white light will seal their psychic toxicity so it won't leak out.

Pour salt on their image, as much as you want.

Say aloud:

"I am cleansed from their wrongdoings and I ask the universe to help them find a way back to truth, honor, and integrity."

Blow the salt away. Drink the water and blow out the candle.

Throw out the picture (do not burn it).

BUSINESS VAMPIRES

Ever feel used? Slimed? Spent—after spending time with someone? If so, you've been consorting with a business vampire. You won't die from the experience, but you won't have the energy to do anything productive, either.

Business vampires sap you of your strength and creativity, leaving them feeling feeling fresh and invigorated. These clever creatures can creep up on you in almost any setting. You have to be pretty smart to realize you're being drained—usually it's not apparent until it's all over. They can pop up anywhere, from your assistant to your boss to the person in the mail room. The key to their success is the time you give them and how open you are to their influence.

If you are astute enough to realize you've got a vampire in your midst, set up some psychic boundaries.

- Close off your crown center and your power center.
- Take deep breaths (sigh) to keep your energy going.
- Stop talking and ask questions back.

If you've been zapped by a vampire, you can revitalize yourself by doing some elemental amplifiers, like increasing your earth element if you feel spacey and detached, or revving up your fire to get your energy going. This takes time and is not very convenient if you're in a small workspace. Consider yourself wounded for the day and don't put too much pressure on yourself.

If you were a willing victim, the vampire will be back the next time he or she needs a fix of energy. Protect yourself more skillfully and that unpleasant being will be forced to look for more fertile feeding grounds.

For constant protection, carry a small piece of onyx with you at all times, and get into the habit of throwing white light around yourself whenever you talk to someone. You might consider wearing a little mirror or medal to ward off evil. Always breathe your power in and exhale toxicity out (visualize inhaling white light and exhaling smog or soot).

SCREAMERS

Who can stand to be in a work environment filled with shrieks and screams? It's not only unprofessional, it's also counterproductive and unnerving. Some industries are just made for screamers, like the trading floor of the commodities exchange or boot camp, yet screamers seem to find their way into many different professions.

A screamer goes into action under circumstances of fear and vulnerability, or in other words, when he or she is threatened or under pressure. It can happen in almost any industry, from accounting to broadcasting, and there's almost no way to predict how or when it's going to occur. Screamers also tend to use their vocal cords just because it feels good; there's nothing like a good tantrum to cleanse every ounce of frustration. In fact, what they're doing is using their throat chakra to expel negativity instead of using salt in the shower—therapeutic for them, unhealthy for you. Some scream because somewhere along the way they learned that screaming was the only way to get their energy going and to actually be heard.

The most important thing you can do for screamers is not listen. Don't take in their energy (it's likely to be toxic), don't participate in their hysteria, and don't show fear. If you do, you will encourage the screamers to scream again—you're showing them that it works.

When a screamer starts on a rampage, you need to protect yourself psychically.

1. Surround yourself with a bubble of white or pink light.
2. Drape your arm over your power center.
3. Evoke a psychic shield by sending the image of bullet-proof glass before you.
4. Walk away. The screamer will follow, probably screaming more. When he or she takes a breath, say your piece. I suggest you put the gist of this into your own words:

"Are you finished? Can I put you on mute for a second? I respond better to calm requests. I'm not made for boot camp. Please try to talk to me like a human being—I'm apt to respond much better if you do."

Lace your message with a smile or some humor if you can, and you'll lighten the impact. Screamers don't like to be told to shut up, and they especially don't know how to respond to good nature or a sense of humor.

Reality check: Screaming is abusive. If you are working with your psychic power, you don't take abuse; you don't have to. If the screamer won't stop screaming at you, get out of that job, get away from that client, get someone else to take it over. Your power cannot thrive there.

Interestingly, I've seen screamers discriminate between whom they can scream at and whom they can't. Lay the ground rules for how you want to be treated anytime you want to—you are the more powerful.

BLAMERS

Did something go wrong? I can practically hear the children in a game of tag say, "Not it!"

Everyone runs across those despicable creatures who pass the buck to anyone who'll accept it. These low-level corporate creeps have no spines. They don't have the courage to own up to their part in a problem situation, which makes a lot of work for everyone else around them.

Blamers don't understand accountability or integrity and spend more time covering their tracks than fixing a problem.

If you're a boss and you see blaming or finger-pointing going on, put a stop to it at once. Don't try to find out who did it, just concentrate on fixing the problem. If the issue is really important, or if it rests heavily on one person or a few people, deal with it face-to-face, without onlookers. Humiliating those who make mistakes will breed a fleet of finger-pointers and buck-passers.

When you're the one someone is trying to finger, enact your psychic power to protect you. This will give you time to get your immediate anger or fear out of the way. You need clarity to proceed. Typically, you'll find out that you're being implicated accidentally or through tip-offs. Most finger-pointers don't point in public.

With your power, you need to hand the responsibility back to the wrongdoer. Either confront him or her directly if appropriate, or do it by memo or on paper, and copy anyone you want to. You're not finger-pointing, you're just helping this poor slob out of a jam.

The note should be written with clarity and friendliness: "Just want to extend any help I can give you with your situation. If there's anything I can do, let me know." No need to go into details, lest you sound defensive. The purpose of this memo is just to hand the psychic "shit" back to its owner.

1. Sit at your desk with the memo.
2. Hold one of your power objects in your hand.
3. Open your power center.
4. Send your power into the paper.

With your power center open, hand the memo to interoffice mail.

If you are in part (but not wholly) responsible, do the same thing, but include a sentence in the note about your part. Own up to your piece; it's more powerful when you do.

PSYCHIC BRIDGE BURNING

One of the strictest rules of business is to never burn bridges. Never insult a measly mail boy who never delivers your mail, because he may end up being one of the most powerful people in your firm (no kidding). Never uncork your frustration with your boss in drunken anger at the Christmas party. Never think that you're rid of people just because you leave that company—they or their evil twin will end up in the office next to you at your next job. Never, never do any bridge burning; and then, never say never.

Now that I've tied your hands up pretty tightly, just what can you do when you are fed up to the teeth with the crap someone else keeps handing you? You can energetically eradicate them from your life. They may still be there, but they won't be able to get to you.

Psychic bridge burning either blows your tormentor's karma clear away from you or—and this does happen—it clears the connection with that person so that you establish a healthier relationship. By consciously letting go of the villain in your life, you destroy your role as a victim, too. This means that if the person reappears, you get to do things differently.

Psychic bridge burning is also a great release for you if you feel particularly hostile toward someone. I know that I've been tormented by petty personalities in the past, and the very fact that someone got the better of me used to torture me silly. Once I burned a psychic bridge, I felt a lot better because I just didn't care anymore. I could even laugh about it, and when humor returns, you know you're healing.

PSYCHIC BRIDGE-BURNING EXERCISE

Take a piece of plain paper. Write the name of the person you would like to dissociate from. Use coloring tools if you want to, such as crayons, markers, colored pencils. Write down as many situations or circumstances this person was responsible for in your life. It is useful to color your anger as you do so.

When you are through, place the paper in your sink. Light it on fire, and allow it to burn as thoroughly as possible. If you find that parts of the paper won't burn, relight them. This is a sign that the bridge is not burning with ease, and that the person might struggle to stay a part of your life. Don't panic. Wait a few weeks and then do it again.

Take the ashes from the sink and throw them out your window or into the trash outside of your home. Wash any remains down your sink, and pour salt down the drain to clear any negativity that may have gotten stuck.

I've burned psychic bridges so well I've never run into the person again (so far) and I like it that way.

My client Kris had been constantly shown up by a competitive executive in her group meetings, and she was dying to give him a piece of her mind.

Instead of embarrassing herself in front of her other colleagues, she tried the bridge-burning technique. She described feeling exhausted afterward, as if she just got tired of raging against him. In subsequent situations, she didn't rise to his bait; she reported that it felt more like he didn't exist. She became more at home with her own power and much less sensitive to him.

Her tormentor ended up taking a job on the opposite coast. That company then merged and the guy lost his job, Kris told me matter-of-factly. But that's not really about bridge burning, that's karmic justice.

A WORD ON KARMIC JUSTICE

I wish I could tell you that every jerk who ever did you wrong was going to get it in the end. Actually, they probably do, but we are not often privy to it.

I personally consider that karmic justice occurs when the villain in question meets an end fitting to his crimes, like a rapist getting prostate cancer and being rendered impotent for many painful years, or like an embezzler who loses all the money he steals by someone else stealing from him.

However, life doesn't usually hand out such neat and tidy cause-and-effects. You could find that the crook who got away with stealing your idea now wields even more power, money, and prestige than he or she had before. Whether it's now or later (and it might end up being much later, like the next lifetime) he or she is going to pay a price for it. Trust me.

Just beware that karmic justice rarely happens in our line of sight. Whatever you do, don't hang around waiting to see when or if someone gets his or her just deserts. It's a waste of your precious time, and it gives him or her the upper hand yet again. Try to trust the universe to come up with a way to teach this devil the meaning of trust and integrity.

WHEN YOU SCREW UP

Yes, it happens. We all make mistakes, sometimes we even act with surprisingly bad judgment. But before you step before the firing squad, consult these tips for dealing with crises and confrontations.

Prepare to Take the Blame

Because you're not going to pass the buck or lie your way out of your problem, you need to formally acknowledge your fault in a problem situation. If you do so with your power on and pride intact, you won't carry sticky karma with you afterward. You will also inspire others to act similarly when their turn comes, which will minimize the number of blamers or liars out there.

1. Sit quietly, relax your breathing.
2. With each inhale, breathe space and light into your heart center.
3. With each exhale, breathe bright yellow light out of your solar plexus power center.
4. Continue to do this for a full minute.
5. Carry a power object, charm, or amulet with you that connects you to a feeling of hope, freedom, or safety. Try a smooth rock for security, a charm you made for success, or an amulet that supports your confidence.
6. Inhale the scent of lavender just before your meeting.

It may be a good idea to practice what you want to say before you face the music. Clarity and calmness will contribute to the success of this difficult endeavor.

If anger, disgust, dismay, or stony silence meet you, stay centered and calm. Evoke whatever psychic shields you need to, including protecting your power center. You may be more at ease in dealing with this than others.

Furthermore, if you become the target of wrath or abuse, stop it in its tracks. Say your piece and leave. Let them vent without you. Your fate is in their hands, but your power is in yours.

Difficult situations are very revealing. It's an opportunity to show you how much integrity your company has. If they react in a powerful way, with clarity and composure, you'll be comfortable with the resolution, whatever it is.

If not, you may think about leaving—that is, if it's still your choice.

Keep Your Perspective

Just a brief word on the motives behind the actions that cause you pain, intentionally or not. Please remember that those who step on your toes and take your ideas, your money, or your goodwill are doing so because they don't think they can do it on their own. Although I do believe there is evil out there, I don't think that every wrong that is done to us is the devil's work. In fact, most of the difficult things that happen to us can be used to better ourselves, so in hindsight they become positive learning experiences.

It is appropriate and often necessary to keep in mind that evildoers may be in pain, and that they live in a world of diminished potential. They just don't get the fact that you can be happy, successful, and nice. They've learned their convoluted method of getting ahead from someone else, and that's how it gets passed on. It is important for you not to participate in their negative cycle, so that you can at least keep it from spreading even further.

If you realize that you are the one who did something wrong, be sure to forgive yourself. The most powerful people allow for imperfection—they learn from it and they move on.

❧ 8 ❧

EXECUTIVE ORACLES

It would be great to have a look into the future. You could know stock prices, executive decisions, sales figures, who's coming and going. Unfortunately, there is no crystal ball that can show you precisely what will take place tomorrow. However, there are a few power tools and methods that can provide you with a peek into the *probable future*—as close as you can get to the real thing.

THE PROBABLE FUTURE

Here's an important distinction: Seers and oracles in the movies seem to predict precise future events. In reality, they can't. Oracles do exist, but they only predict what is *likely to happen*.

❧

Because the future hasn't yet happened, it can almost always be shifted. There is no way of knowing exactly what will happen until it happens.

❧

Although you may be disappointed to learn that you can't see the exact future, there are many reasons to be grateful that it is not yet etched in stone. Believe me, you want to be able to shape and shift your future—that way you can consciously make it better.

Your future is constantly forming, and has been ever since you took your first breath, when your parents decided what to call you, when you went home from the hospital. Your present is a direct result of every decision that has been made for you since you were born and every decision you've made even before you can remember.

Adding to this complicated progression of choices, your present is also a result of decisions made by many people around you.

WHY BOTHER WITH THE PROBABLE FUTURE? When you have the opportunity to make a conscious decision about something important in your life, you might as well get as much input as you can. Ask an oracle to give you insight or support, and consider its information with your head and your heart.

✪

Never allow an oracle to make a decision for you. It is there to help you look further into your own intuition for the right answer.

✪

Don't look to an oracle to predict the exact future. Look to it for guidance, likelihood, and insight. Then act according to what you want—to change the future, prepare for it, or welcome it.

ORACLES

Oracles are fascinating tools, with a long history of use, dating as far back as humankind has had time to ponder the future. You may remember learning in school of the famous Oracle of Delphi. She (history presumes she was a priestess) "saw" the future and predicted events. She most likely had a gift of clairvoyance, which we don't all enjoy, but fortunately you don't need to find a priestess in these modern times. You can seek your own intuitive guidance with your power tools.

Practically all of us played with a Ouija board or a Magic Eight Ball at some point in our youth. I don't recommend them per se, but there are plenty of other easy-to-use sources to help you identify opportunities, obstacles, wins, and losses in your future.

Each oracle has a distinct character and method of operating. You'll no doubt find one that suits you.

- The *I Ching* is a well-respected Chinese method that interprets the hexagrams you form with coin tosses. This ancient oracle is so old that it is believed to predate recorded history. The *I Ching*'s original text is translated into English, but its density and meaning can be prohibitively complex. After all, the way of life and mythology in Bronze Age China is not easily applicable to our culture. Instead of the original *I Ching* (which some purists prefer), you may want to use one of the more modern books available in your bookstore or library. There are many versions—for example, some are more focused on feminine attributes, while some are fashioned for quick readings, and some versions focus on life transitions. As with any oracle, use equal parts intellect and intuition to guide you. This means, if you like it, if you understand it, and if it feels right, it's for you.

- **Tarot cards** allow you to choose a reading from seventy-eight cards whose numbers, symbols, and archetypes tell the story of your situation. Most people believe the tarot originated in the ancient Egyptian culture, where different life phases or "archetypes" were identified with the path of the soul. The numbered cards and symbols may have come later, and the first printed tarot cards are from pre-Renaissance Italy. Although the form of tarot cards has changed over the years, the basic archetypes are still the same and can tell a profoundly insightful story of the future.

- **Runes** are a recently popularized tool traced to Viking civilization, which provide insight into life passages. The Vikings originally used these basic etchings on their swords, in their homes, and on their boats as symbols for protection, success, or transformation. Today's runes are composed of these same glyphs, reinterpreted for our use to navigate through life's sometimes troubled waters.

- You can even use a favorite book to give you insight with the technique called **bibliomancy.** This practice is popular among Bible lovers. It involves asking a book to provide the answer to a specific concern or question.

I recommend experimenting with different oracles until you find the one or two that work best for you. I'm not a big *I Ching* user; I favor the tarot cards simply because it's easier for me to read them than the other oracles. My friend Emily uses bibliomancy regularly to let her know how a meeting will go, while some of my clients stick to their runes for routine answers to their daily business questions. You'll know which oracle works best for you only after you've sampled it. If you find yourself confused or uncomfortable with a certain oracle, try another.

You may even find that you use different oracles for different occasions. When my clients have deeper issues they are wrestling with, like making a career change, I usually have them pick a rune, which I use myself for "heavy duty" questions. One of my clients picks a rune every morning to tell him what quality he is going to work with that day—he obviously has a lighter relationship with them. He told me he uses the *I Ching* when he has a more important question to ask.

Finding an oracle you feel comfortable with that does not

intimidate you with its complexity or its answers is most important. Try a few of them to see which one or two you like. Borrow a friend's deck of cards or try out a sample of runes in a store for a start.

Use Them, Don't Abuse Them

Oracles exist to help you find answers to questions in your life. But what happens if you don't like the answer? You can't make an oracle "take back" what it tells you.

I've argued with my tarot cards more than once, and I've seen others toss out a perfectly good reading for "the best of two out of three," which, of course, doesn't work anyway. You can't change your probable future with just another shuffle or coin toss. Only your action and psychic power (sending energy into the future) have the potential to influence your future.

&

When you consult an oracle, make sure you are open to the answer, even if it's not the one you want.

&

My client Yolande was going through a tough time at work and wanted to know if she was going to keep her job. She was working in a firm that was undergoing a merger and she had no idea if her position would be eliminated. She asked her tarot cards and got a card that indicated financial hardship. She asked the runes and they also implied a time of pain and adversity. She didn't like these answers and kept asking—but they didn't change. Once she got used the idea that she was likely to be laid off, she took action and started looking for a new job. Her position was terminated only a week later, but at least she was not caught off guard.

It's no fun to confront an unpleasant outcome, but no amount of doing an oracle over again will change it. Many oracles tend to get annoyed if you ask the same question too often. The *I Ching* has a way of telling you to stop asking; tarot cards will start showing you gibberish (or the Fool card), and the runes will tell you to stop taking action. In other words, you can't argue with an oracle.

Here are some steps you can take to ensure that you are ready to hear what your oracle has to say:

1. Ground yourself before asking the question. Place your feet firmly on the ground, take a deep breath in, and exhale slowly.
2. Clearly articulate the question you want to ask. Yes/no questions don't work very well. Try to ask for insight into a situation or ask what the future of your project holds.
3. Choose your card or rune, or conduct your coin toss with as much calm and clarity as you can muster. Do not pull an answer when you're in a panic—your fear could be dictating the outcome.

When my client Hal pulled a tarot card to see if his next book project would be a success, the card indicated that hidden events, secrecy, and darkness were clouding the outcome. Hal got very nervous about this; he sensed his publishers were not as enthusiastic as he had hoped they'd be, which was precisely why he'd asked the question in the first place. I asked him to pull another card for more insight. This one represented a man of influence who would carry a project to its fruition. Hal was concerned that he would have to promote the book on his own, an expensive and time-draining effort.

The cards were fairly accurate, but Hal's interpretation didn't hold. Hal's publishers decided not to go through with his book at all, but his agent (a man) sold it to another publishing company where it was more enthusiastically produced. The cards were right, but the story Hal concocted to fit the cards was wrong. This, unfortunately, is not unusual.

We are all like Hal: remarkably bad at seeing how the oracles' predictions might play out. Hal immediately thought he was the man who'd have to go to bat for his project, when in fact he had nothing to do with it. Get used to this. The oracles will tell you the essential outcome but they won't tell you the story of how you'll arrive there. You might fall into the trap of believing you know just how events will play out, and you may even see things to be worse than they are. Events almost always happen differently from how we imagine, but most often the oracles are right. Don't try to read more into the answer; the trick with an oracle is to trust that it is right and work with that knowledge.

If the outcome is good, allow events to come to pass as they will. If you don't care for the outcome, be on the lookout for ways you may be able to shift it (with your power tools) or to prepare for it without too much discomfort.

Appropriate Questions for Oracles

Stay away from yes/no questions. Oracles are best used for insight, not to tell you what to do. If you want to know the outcome of a situation, consult your oracle for the story of the likely future. You'll get a feel for "yes" or "no" and much more. Try asking these questions:

Am I on the right career path?

Should I make a change in my career path now?

Should I ask for a promotion?

Is this a good opportunity?

Is this person good to work with?

How is my company doing?

Will this project come to fruition?

How are my sales going to play out this year?

Is this offer competitive?

Will this product have a fighting chance?

What kind of challenges are ahead?

What do I need to work on to get better at my job?

The I Ching: The Book of Changes

The *I Ching* is actually a system of sixty-four line diagrams called hexagrams, each carrying a different meaning. You can form these hexagrams by tossing three coins (or, if you're a purist, you can use yarrow stalks) six times and interpreting each coin toss as either a whole line or a broken line depending on the combination of coins. The hexagram you form will "translate" into a Chinese metaphor, or story that is an answer to your question.

Most often, an *I Ching* divination will require you to toss three coins (pennies are fine) six times and interpret them as follows:

Three heads: solid line (_____)

Three tails: broken line (_____ _____)

Two heads, one tail: solid line (_____)

Two tails, one head: broken line (_____ _____)

For divination, you can use the *I Ching* to "answer" a question for you.

Each toss is a line of your hexagram, starting at the bottom. In some readings, you make a secondary hexagram derived from the first, bringing you another layer of insight.

An *I Ching* book will guide you through the interpretation of the hexagrams you form. This takes time to do, so the reading takes on a reverent, ritualistic quality. The *I Ching* can also be long-winded, so don't look for a quick fix. You will need to consider the message given and apply it to your original question.

Don't ask the *I Ching* the same question too many times. It will tell you to "shut up" very politely but very firmly. Ask the kind of question that can be answered in "essay" form.

"Should I consider this new job?"

"Does this idea has any value?"

"How can I make this transition work smoother?"

"What kind of stance should I take in this negotiation?"

When my client Todd was waiting for what he considered an overdue promotion, he got restless and slightly nervous; he worried that perhaps it wouldn't happen. He considered bringing it up with his boss, but he didn't want to appear insecure. Instead, he got his *I Ching* out to "see" what was going on.

His hexagram was called "Increase," indicating that he would, indeed, gain or benefit soon. Just seeing these words relaxed him. He admitted, though, that still nothing had happened after a week, so he did the *I Ching* again. He got a similar message, "Advancement," which advised to wait patiently for advancement rather than push for it. He did receive his promotion shortly thereafter.

Another client, Ronnie, asked the *I Ching* to find out if her client would be financially responsible and pay her on time. She tossed her *I Ching* and found her hexagram was called "Family." At first, she didn't understand how it applied, but as she read the interpretation thoroughly, she found the phrase "woman must persevere." She took that to mean she had to stay on top of her billing and remind the clients to pay. As it turned out, they were occasionally late but always responded to her calls.

The Tarot

Tarot cards are one of my favorite oracles for use with clients because I have a deck that really works for me, I find them easy to interpret, and I enjoy the ritual of choosing a card. For some people, however, they are hard to interpret or even scary. If that's the case for you, try a different oracle.

I advise people who want to use a tarot deck to try the "Devil" test to see if they like it. The Devil card is a major arcana card that represents temptation, something you judge to be "bad" for you, or something that you'll have to "pay for." This can mean that having a martini at a business lunch is not the best idea because you'll pay for it with a headache, or it can mean that the deal you are about to make has hidden strings attached—but you're tempted to do it anyway. Look in the booklet that comes with the deck and see what it says. In some decks, this card is really nasty, implying that you are a no-good materialist or that you'll be punished for what you want. Forget any deck that judges too harshly. If you can live with the interpretation provided for the Devil card, you can probably live with the deck. Then just make sure you feel good about the pictures (I hate the ones with lots of swords killing people) and you'll almost certainly find the deck useful.

A standard tarot deck consists of seventy-eight cards, with fifty-six in the minor arcana and twenty-two in the major arcana. You will find the fifty-six minor arcana cards similar to our modern-day playing cards. There are four suits, fourteen cards to a suit. In fact, today's playing cards can be read like tarot cards. (I'll explain how to later in this book.)

The four suits of the minor arcana are Swords, Wands, Coins, and Cups. Sometimes Coins are called Pentacles, and Cups are called Hearts. You'll know by looking at the card.

Each suit relates to the elements—fire, earth, air, or water—and their respective qualities.

Suit	Element	Quality/Power
Wands *Clubs*	Fire	Passion/ Aggression
Coins/Pentacles *Diamonds*	Earth	Prosperity/ Health
Swords *Spades*	Air	Ideas/ Communications
Cups *Hearts*	Water	Relationships/ Emotions

The cards of the minor arcana build from one to ten, then Page, Knight, Queen, King. The Page and Queen are considered feminine cards, while the Knight and King are masculine. Each card is associated with a different meaning. Some of the cards are more easily understood; for instance, the Queen of Hearts looks like a love card and the King of Wands often looks like an aggressive man.

The twenty-two major arcana cards have no association with modern playing cards. They are representative of different archetypal situations, some being personal life stages and others being circumstances. Again, some of these cards are easier to read, like the Lovers, or Justice. However, try not to immediately assign a negative meaning to a card. The Death card, for instance, means change, and the Devil card asks you to beware of your own judgments; getting those cards is not a threat that you're doomed to live in hell.

The major arcana is actually the story of the soul's journey. The first card (0) is the Fool, meaning open potential. This would be an excellent card to pull if you wanted to start a new business, but perhaps not great if you're trying to close a specific deal. It is too open, implying that things are not ready to come to completion. The next card is the Trickster or Magician. My entrepreneurial clients almost always pull that card—it is an indication of an inventive personality.

Like the minor arcana, each card is described in a booklet that allows you to interpret for your situation. Every card has an upside and a downside, so read both to be able to apply your intuitive knowledge.

Sometimes tarot cards seem too convoluted for business, so I've taken time to translate a general tarot deck for business purposes. Check out the chart on pages 215–17.

You can do several kinds of readings with tarot cards. A long reading would be a ten-card Celtic cross. This kind of spread would describe your past, present, and future situation, what you need to do, what you'll get from others, and what's in the way of what you want. The Celtic cross is an excellent way to see how well your cards speak to you, because this reading will most likely cover your question fully and accurately.

Short readings with the tarot are even easier. Just do a three-card pick for past, present, and future, and see a snapshot of your situation. For quick insight into a project, just pick one tarot card.

I often use one card to help identify projects with the most potential. For instance, my client Betsey didn't know whether to continue her freelance work, take a part-time job, or take a full-time job. She picked three cards, one for each option.

Freelance work: Seven of Coins
Part-time work: Star
Full-time work: Tower

Betsey's cards indicated that the freelance work was risky, as indicated by the Seven of Coins. The Star card for part-time work showed hope and light during a dark time—not a bad option. The Tower card meant a full-time job could bring about unpleasant or unexpected disruption. The reading clarified Betsey's ambivalence. She was tired of the uncertainty of her freelance life but wasn't sure she could pop back into a nine-to-five life.

The part-time situation was the most palatable for her, and the cards just helped to point it out.

Choosing a Tarot Deck

Like the *I Ching*, tarot decks come in many different varieties. It is vitally important that you choose a deck that speaks to you. My first deck was beautiful, but didn't really give me any useful information. The second deck I found became my favorite.

I have one deck for my all-purpose, everyday-life questions and another deck I consider more sacred, for when I need more insight or the questions are heavy. I even have a deck to use when I want a change of insight. Each deck will interpret the same symbols with subtle differences, and you may find that one suits your mood more than another.

TAROT TRANSLATED FOR BUSINESS
Major Arcana

NUMBER	TRADITIONAL TAROT NAME	EXECUTIVE TAROT NAME
Zero	Fool	Potential
One	Magician	Entrepreneur
Two	Virgin	Intuition
Three	Empress	Feminine power
Four	Emperor	Masculine power
Five	Pope	Hierarchy
Six	Lovers	Partnership
Seven	Chariot	Victory
Eight	Strength	Strength
Nine	Hermit	Introspection
Ten	Wheel of Fortune	Fate
Eleven	Justice	Justice
Twelve	Hanged Man	Surrender

Thirteen	Death	Transformation
Fourteen	Temperance	Patience
Fifteen	Devil	Expediency
Sixteen	Tower	Disruption
Seventeen	Star	Hope
Eighteen	Moon	Hidden elements
Nineteen	Sun	Vitality
Twenty	Judgment	Forgiveness
Twenty-one	The World	Totality

Minor Arcana and Playing Cards*

WANDS/CLUBS		COINS/DIAMONDS	
One of Wands	Initiative	One of Coins	New enterprise
Two of Wands	Excitement	Two of Coins	Setting up
Three of Wands	Work	Three of Coins	Firstfruits
Four of Wands	Work harmony	Four of Coins	Stability
Five of Wands	Stress	Five of Coins	Small loss
Six of Wands	Work synchronicity	Six of Coins	Profit
Seven of Wands	Challenges	Seven of Coins	Risk
Eight of Wands	Team effort	Eight of Coins	Conservative gain
Nine of Wands	Force	Nine of Coins	Gains
Ten of Wands	Overkill	Ten of Coins	Topping out
Page of Wands*	Young creative female	Page of Coins*	Young practical female
Knight of Wands*	Young creative male	Knight of Coins	Young practical male

*In playing cards, the Jack serves as both the Knight and the Page, so there is no gender difference in the youthful face card.

Queen of Wands	Mature creative female	Queen of Coins	Mature practical female
King of Wands	Mature creative male	King of Coins	Mature practical male

SWORDS/SPADES		CUPS/HEARTS	
One of Swords	A new idea	One of Hearts	A new feeling
Two of Swords	An offer	Two of Hearts	Partnership
Three of Swords	Common sense	Three of Hearts	Shared joy
Four of Swords	Reflection	Four of Hearts	Serenity
Five of Swords	Conflict	Five of Hearts	Tension
Six of Swords	Clarity	Six of Hearts	Understanding
Seven of Swords	Imagination/ obscurity	Seven of Hearts	Inattention
Eight of Swords	Thoughtfulness	Eight of Hearts	Self-control/ depth
Nine of Swords	Facing fears	Nine of Hearts	Satisfaction
Ten of Swords	Intellectual achievement	Ten of Hearts	Gratitude
Page of Swords*	A young intellectual female	Page of Hearts*	A young, emotional female
Knight of Swords*	A young intellectual male	Knight of Hearts	A young emotional male
Queen of Swords	A mature intellectual female	Queen of Hearts	A mature emotional female
King of Swords	A mature intellectual male	King of Hearts	A mature emotional male

Dealer's Choice: Reading Playing Cards

More than one businessperson I know has a pack of playing cards in their desk, and not for a quick game of Solitaire, either. You can use a regular playing card to pick for insight into a situation at work. You just need to know the suits and what the numbers mean. The preceding chart serves as a guide for readings. You'll be surprised at how quickly you can learn.

Connie, a producer for a popular talk show, is always looking for new angles for stories. Her job is high-pressure and she is driven to succeed in making each of her segments unique, so she puts additional pressure on herself. As is the nature of her business, there's been more than one instance when a guest has canceled at the last minute or she has been scooped by a rival talk show.

Always in search of an edge, Connie got tired of being surprised by her competitors, so she started consulting an oracle fairly regularly. I taught her to read an ordinary playing card deck and she loved it. She began to consult her cards weekly. At first she turned up cards like the Six of Wands (profit) and Three of Coins (firstfruits) and figured all was well. The third week, she pulled a card that meant a risk (Seven of Diamonds), and the next day, a small loss (Five of Diamonds). She took precautions to ensure that her bookings were confirmed, but she also took steps to cover herself by starting work on another segment idea. By Thursday, she pulled the Five of Swords (conflict) and her main guest canceled. She was surprised by how accurately the playing cards had tracked the story and impressed by how adequately she had prepared. Her backup story was produced the following week, keeping her lost time to a minimum. She now consults her cards daily.

Pulling a tarot card or playing card from a shuffled deck can also give you a quick look into the status of a project or a business situation. I often have my clients state what their projects are aloud and then pull a card to see how it comments on their work. You can also use the cards to give you week-by-week or month-by-month projections to track what the future is likely to hold. Remember, the cards reveal the main quality of that project, week, or month, but they won't tell you how or why that will arise. You are best off just knowing that a certain project may be delayed, or that in three weeks you'll be experiencing a big opportunity or loss—depending on what the cards say. What you probably won't be able to project is exactly how it will come about.

I did a month-by-month projection for a client not long ago. He is a retail stockbroker who was considering getting into institutional sales. We looked into the next three months with some playing cards and saw the following:

June	One of Diamonds	New enterprise
July	Five of Swords	Conflict
August	Eight of Hearts	Self-control, depth

We discussed this spread and he thought it made sense. Although he was focused on doing something new in the month of June, he thought there might be some difficulty in making the transition (conflict) and that he would want to rethink changing the focus of his work.

You can use your cards for insight into any question or to project into your future, but try to resist absolute questions (will I get this job, will my raise be ten percent, and so on). You can't expect a conclusive answer.

Bibliomancy

Bibliomancy offers a very quick fix to any question you might have and can be performed without great ceremony, but you may find its answer incomplete. *Bibliomancy* is allowing a random sentence or passage in a book to guide you to an answer to your question. Many people still use the Bible in this way: Ask a question out loud, ask the Lord to tell you what you need to know, stick your finger in the Bible on a random page and a random line. Read it aloud and see if it makes sense.

As often as the answer may seem incomplete, you may also be surprised by how enlightening this can be. Obviously, you need to use a book that offers the kind of text that "speaks" to you, and it is best if you have a relationship with the book itself. My friend Gina uses her grandfather's dictionary, and always seems to land on a word that makes sense to her question. Another friend of mine uses a huge book on mythology, so that she can see which story pertains to her question.

Bibliomancy offers you very easy access to an oracle. Just be sure that the book you choose has the kind of text that can offer you advice. I know people who use novels (*The Old Man and the Sea*), "alternative" philosophy books (*The Tibetan Book of Living and Dying*). I, like Gina, use a dictionary. You can try different books until you hit on one that "speaks" to you. Consider books that have touched you in some way, that taught you something new, or that presented you with a philosophy you admired.

Runes

A few years ago, runes became a (re)popularized method of divining information about the future. They had not been used for more than three hundred years until Ralph Blum, an archaeologist, resurrected them for divination. He found they could be used for insight into life passages and spent years working with them and researching their origins. He reinterpreted glyphs from the old Viking civilizations and found deeper and more up-to-date meanings with respect to modern life's events. Today you can buy a bag of runes, smooth white stones with runic glyphs etched into them, in your local bookstore or New Age shop. One rune looks like an *X*, while another is a simple vertical line.

Some look like the English alphabet. They are primitive in their look but not in their meanings.

The runes are fairly heavy oracles, not just because you use a bag of stones, but for their interpretations. They are not to be played with lightly. I find runes best for those events or decisions that require deeper insight, such as when you are considering a career change, your company is being sold or taken over, or you feel that winds of change are approaching but you don't know why. Runes work well when you need some support for trying times, if you get laid off, or if you're just being creatively or psychically challenged. Their insights will give you much to think about, more than the brief replies from tarot cards or the descriptive passages of the *I Ching*. You also won't need to pick more than one rune to get a decisive answer. Runes are very powerful symbols that can add to your personal power today, just as they did in ancient Norse culture.

Live Psychics: Readings for Sale?

There are many excellent and highly skilled psychics, readers, and practitioners out there for you to call upon if you want some professional psychic input. Of course, because I have my own clientele, I support the idea.

You may want to use a professional in consulting an oracle when you are very emotionally interested in the outcome. An oracle will respond to your question whether you ask it directly or through a professional, but when your emotions are charged, you may not interpret the answer clearly if you try to do so solo. Your emotions can also override your psychic energy so much that you could pull a card representing your fear or hopefulness rather than an objective view of the situation. When you are very worried, such as about losing a job, or if you feel your will for success is extra strong, you may need someone else to keep an objective eye on your future.

There are some people who give psychic readings over the phone or by mail. You may choose to use one of these readers, and you might even get a good reading. Plenty of people swear by their phone psychics, but I just can't help encouraging you to attend a reading in person. You will get much more out of it, not to mention the fact that the person doing the reading will get a better connection to your psychic energy.

If you do choose to go to a professional reader, there are a few things you need to know. *Caveat emptor*—buyer beware—applies in all transactions, particularly in psychic readings.

1. Before you commit to a reading, speak to the person on the phone, if not in person, to make sure you connect with him or her. If you don't, find someone else. There is no reason for you to be uncomfortable; this could color the information you receive.

2. If a reader tries to bully or coerce you into a reading, saying something like "You aura is very dirty. I should clear it for you or you might attract the evil eye," say good-bye. Even if your aura is filthy, you want to avoid going to people who try to scare you into paying them.

3. If it's too expensive for your purse, walk away. I am always shocked at what some people pay (and what some people charge) for psychic readings. If you feel the reader is good and you are comfortable with the amount, it's your call. Good readings come from your rapport with the reader and the reader's psychic ability; money doesn't guarantee success.

4. If any psychic reader uses the word *never* in answering an important question, don't take what he or she says too seriously. There is no such thing as an absolute in this world, and people who use absolutes are usually not that open psychically or emotionally.

5. Don't believe everything you hear. Only you know if the reading makes sense. Readers who insist on being right all

the time probably won't be, and can make you feel power-less if you don't validate what they say.

If you've decided to go ahead and find a reader, here's how to do it.

- Ask a friend for a recommendation.
- Go to a New Age bookstore and look at the bulletin board, then do some phone interviews.
- Get your local paper and check out the ads.

However you come to the reader of your choice, listen with both your heart and your head. Ask questions when you don't understand something. If you are very nervous or afraid, your fear can block the reader. Be sure to say so if you're uncomfortable or you don't want to talk about something. Use your power tools to stay in control.

MORE APPLICATIONS OF ORACLES
The Stock Market

The stock market is actually just one big psychic realm. What makes a stock go up and down is based purely on the belief we put into it—do we believe that the company is going to be successful or not? If so, we buy the stock and "bet" that it will go up. If many other people feel this, too, the stock actually does go up in value as a result of demand—large-group belief.

There are lots of psychic power tool users in the stock market. Astrology seems to be the leading method. You can hire a financial astrologer to chart your investment course and even recommend stocks. These professionals have both a financial background and a practical business background, and this is serious business.

Or, if you are just a small investor or want to play the market for fun, you can use some of the oracles presented here to guide you to a stock or investment that's best for you. Just ask a specific question to the oracle at hand and see what you get back.

"Is this company managed well?"

"Does this stock have growth potential?"

"Can this stock price go up in the next month?"

Be careful not to project too far out with the stock market; I don't go any further than four weeks with a comfortable degree of accuracy. This is because the group psychic energy that constitutes the stock market can shift overnight, depending on factors we cannot foresee (terrorism, the fall of foreign currency, bad crop years, corporate scandals).

My friend Brandt, a stockbroker, uses his *I Ching* to project his sales and income for the month ahead. On the evening of the thirtieth of a month, he sits down, tosses his coins, and looks up his hexagram. He tells me that his forecasts have been very accurate, and he uses his results to gauge how much his personal income will be affected.

Horace, an amateur investor, uses his tarot cards to determine if it is a good time to buy stocks or sell stocks. On the new moon he asks the question "buy?" and on the full moon he asks "sell?" and picks a card. Because his portfolio is small, if he gets the okay to sell, he picks a card to determine which stock should go; if he is buying, he picks a card for each stock he is considering. His system seems to work well for him.

HORACE'S SAMPLE READING
New Moon

Is this a good time to buy a stock?

Tarot Answer: Two of Coins (there is fertile ground for growth).

Which stock should I buy?

Tarot Answer: Stock One—Virgin (not ready yet to bloom);

Stock Two—Moon (not all is known); Stock Three—Two of Fire (excitement).

He went with stock number three, which is now performing conservatively well.

Full Moon

Is this a good time to sell a stock?

Tarot Answer: Devil (although there may be a good price offered on a stock in his current holdings, he may not get the best price for it).

Horace held off selling.

As with any oracle, use it only as a guide.

CAN AN ORACLE BE WRONG?

Yes. Not often, but yes. Oracles are not perfect (the world isn't, either) so they can be wrong at times. Oracles fluctuate with our own psychic energy, our fears, and the choices made in the world around us. Usually, if you are clear on what you are asking, you are likely to get a good answer. More often than not, an oracle will tell you something in a roundabout way, and confound you into thinking it's wrong when it's really right.

For instance, my friend Rozzie applied for a new job as a writer at a magazine, and her experience was only in editing at a children's publishing house. She had good interviews, good connections, and basically good chances of getting the job. She consulted her runes to see if it would happen.

Rozzie chose a three-rune spread, showing past, present, and future. Her question was: "Will I work well at the magazine?"

For her answer she got the rune of breakthrough in the past, the rune of a gateway for the present, and the rune she nicknamed the icicle, or standstill, for the future. It seemed to her that although she had broken into the magazine world and even gotten through the door (gateway), she didn't have a place there (standstill), so it wouldn't work.

She was depressed for about twenty-four hours, at the end of which they called to offer her the job. She did get the job, but she hated it after about a month. She didn't feel comfortable in the environment and knew that she would have to find another job as soon as she got enough experience.

So the oracle was right; it answered her question properly. Rozzie broke through, got the job, and came to a standstill once she got there.

Oracles will sometimes not answer you at all. You may ask something unknowable (like when someone will die) or there may be something so hidden that you are not supposed to know or are not ready to know, be it either positive or negative news. Sometimes it isn't appropriate to know that your boss is going to quit and you'll be promoted into that job. The future may not yet be formed (your boss could be only considering leaving right now). Sometimes things happen very abruptly, too, and no oracle could predict them. After all, we live in a realm of free will and choice, so it makes sense that not everything can be foreseen.

Even I like to listen to Doris Day sing "Que será, será" once in a while. The future isn't always ours to see.

FINAL TIPS FOR
EXECUTIVE MYSTICS

Congratulations! You are now well on your way to becoming a skilled, practiced executive mystic, with a growing sense of your psychic power and how you can effectively influence your path to success.

As you proceed with sharpening your psychic skills, consider some parting words of wisdom.

THE MORE YOU USE IT THE BETTER YOU GET

You may just settle on a few power objects, a charm, and a favorite oracle, and not bother using your power centers or your ability to send energy into the future. You'll still be effective with your efforts, but you won't be using your fullest potential. Try to practice with the exercises throughout the book, and slowly expand your repertoire. You may find that some techniques come in handy for specific facets of your career. For instance, if you begin to deal with more new people, your power wardrobe and your ability to read their psychic energy will become crucial. If you find your work brings you into more risk-taking situations, you may want to use your oracles combined with moon phases for guidance. Remember to use this book as a reference guide to refresh your knowledge and strategically apply different tools to different occasions in order to stack the intuitive deck.

DON'T HOLD ON TO YOUR GOALS TOO TIGHTLY

You may think that you can never be too powerful, but you're wrong. There are some instances where your psychic energy can overwhelm the very opportunity you are trying to manifest. It can be like a fireball trying to light a matchstick—your power will incinerate the opportunity instead of fueling it. You can prevent this by not putting too much energy behind your desire. Do not send energy into your desired future every day, do not push power objects into mounds around your office. Don't get obsessive. Let the opportunity have space to breathe and grow, and nourish it with a healthy dose of your energy. If you need guidelines for this, do just one or two manifesting techniques per goal during every moon cycle. More than that is probably not necessary.

SHARE YOUR WEALTH

There is one tried-and-true way to ensure that your psychic power will stay clear and intact, and that is by giving back to the world in appreciation of what you have been able to create. This is called tithing. An ancient ritual of respect for the harvest, it is part of most world religions.

Your psychic energy is constantly fueled by nature and your relationship to nature. If you take care of living things, you increase your psychic power. When you harvest your goals, it is important to give back, to say thank you to the greater power of manifestation. This psychically retills the soil so that it can remain fertile for more manifestations to come. If you don't take care of your psychic grounds, they may not remain very fertile for very long.

You can tithe in many ways, by giving money you've earned to charity, by giving time as a mentor, or by volunteering. By giving back, by doing something without expecting a reward, you will in turn develop a better relationship to prosperity and have a deeper satisfaction with what you create.

KEEP YOUR BALANCE

It's very easy to get caught up in the thrill of the chase, in making business happen, in seeing your own power manifest. That's all part of using your power tools—just beware of focusing too much on them. Don't let the fruits of your psychic power efforts take over for your brain power, your objectivity, or your sociability. You can't use them as substitutes for thinking clearly, coming up with ideas, seeing through projects, or making new acquaintances. They can help you do all of these things better, but you still have to put your physical and mental energy behind your business efforts.

I've seen some of my clients take to this work like a duck to water, but I've also seen the side effects of leaning too heavily on it. You could end up out of balance—not thinking things through or asking for regular old advice from respected colleagues. Power tools are an excellent supplement to a well-balanced work life, but are not to be used independently of reasonable business behavior.

KEEP YOUR POWER TOOLS TO YOURSELF

If you're worried that your friends or colleagues will judge you for using power tools, don't tell them. Your psychic power is highly individual and has nothing to do with other people. Most of my clients are discreet with their tools because they feel it gives them a competitive edge, but you'd be surprised to learn how many people are using them already.

ABOVE ALL, ENJOY YOUR POWER

A good executive mystic wields power with good humor and a sensible philosophy: If it's meant to be, enjoy it; if not, move on to something else.

Don't tally up your victories or losses and judge your progress. Instead, make an appraisal of your life, the satisfaction you feel, the goals you've met, and the opportunities in front of you. Using your psychic power is a never-ending game. See how far it can take you, and enjoy the process of getting there.

INDEX